STOKE-ON-TRENT
CITY ARCHIVES
Telephone: 01782 238420

STAFFS DUD
TWEMLOW. R. L.

VILLAGE SWALLOWS

BY

REGINALD TWEMLOW

Village Swallows

by

Reginald Twemlow

illustrations

by

Richard Twemlow

FIRST EDITION
1983

Printed in England
by
HART BOULTON & COMPANY LIMITED
Stoke-on-Trent

INTRODUCTION

by John Bates, B.A., M.Phil.

Reginald Twemlow was born at Sandford Hill, Stoke-on-Trent, and educated at
Woodhouse Senior School where he showed great promise at English and
submitted a prize-winning essay in 1934. On leaving school he entered mining
engineering. In 1940 he enlisted into the Irish Guards but later transferred to the
Royal Engineers for which his earlier training had qualified him. He saw active
service in Normandy and Belgium and left the army in 1946. In 1948 he joined
the Staffordshire County Police and served for 25 years, entirely within the Leek
division, and for the greater part as a country policeman. He retired in 1973.

It was in the Staffordshire Police that I first met him, we discovered that we
had a common link through the Irish Guards in which I also served. But we had
another bond; literature. I met him only once a year when we were both on duty
at Mucclestone Races on Easter Saturday. He always saved me a seat on the coach
and our talk turned inevitably on what we had read. He was, and is, an omnivorous
reader. Twemlow had, in 1961, a slim volume of verse to his credit and had been
interviewed on television. He was, so far as I am aware, the first published policeman
poet. It would have been surprising if his muse had deserted him in his retirement,
and though her visits may be less frequent they have not ceased. It was a considerable
honour to be asked to write the introduction to my old friend's volume but a task
that I undertook not without some reservations and with much trepidation, since I
cannot claim to be a literary critic, much less a poet.

Now there are many definitions of poetry. Sir Isaac Newton's is the most
amusing, 'an ingenious sort of nonsense'. Wordsworth has described poetry as
taking 'its origin from emotion recollected in tranquillity', while Hilaire Belloc
declares 'verse is a slow thing to create........it is a secretion of the mind, it is a
pearl that gathers round some irritant and slowly expresses the very essence of
the beauty and of desire that had lain long, potential and unexpressed in the mind
of the man who secretes it'. These will suffice. I have always felt that verse should
be used to hit off that which cannot properly be expressed in prose.

Twemlow's muse is essentially rural and he is on sure ground when he writes
about what he knows. He writes in the framework of rhyme and metre and is
quite untouched by modern fashions. His poems are concerned with nature, wild
life, his beloved Moorlands district and its legends, some of which he has preserved
here in verse. Many of his poems are concerned with what Richard Church called

'the small moments' which are the very stuff of our lives. Twemlow's wry sense of humour shows through and the volume is scattered with epigrams. Memories of childhood, adolescence, his view of sycophants, and, of course the nature poems. These then are the collection of a lifetime of a man who has done a lot of living. The Reg Twemlow I know comes through, and while some of his political judgements may seem a little extreme, and his attack on taxation an echo of Dr. Johnson's famous definition of 'excise' in the dictionary, it is his own voice that speaks through the poems. I have often wondered what impels a man to write. Doctor Johnson said 'none but a fool writes for money', but any poet would testify that for the great majority the writing of verse is a labour of love. The poet writes because he has something that he wishes to say. He hopes also to be remembered. The poem that stands at the end of this volume seems to me to sum it up and Twemlow is at one with the poets in wishing that something of his shall have the power to live and last.

Like all poets Twemlow is a lover of music and the Viennese composers are his favourites.

Croxton.
Eccleshall.

CONTENTS

THE CARDS

The wind blew wild o'er Longnor town
And swept away brown autumn's crown,
And as the sabbath morn wore on
The pale bleak sun so fitful shone.
The bells tolled out their hymnal song
As huddling groups that way did throng.
Each husbandman as was his care
Had left his toil or fireside chair,
And sought the hard bench pews inside
That hallowed place where angels bide.

One row stood empty cold and bare,
Hugh Walker's flock this deed did dare,
And looks and nods were passed around
Their story told without a sound.
Luke Anstey stumbled with the plate
As that great void caused him to wait.
The preacher's voice and eyes were flung
Where neither prayer nor praise was sung.

Where bleak the moorland stretches wide,
Where timid hares and moorcock hide,
And deer leap out with silent stride
Like the Headless Horseman on his ride -
Near Mosscarrs Hill by a tiny stream
The grey stone farm so drab is seen.
Its buildings hung with peeling doors
Show marks of toil by teeth and claws.
The kitchen clean but coldly bare
Seemed homely by the lamp's warm glare.
Beside a table spread with food
Sat six young men - Hugh Walker's brood.

Their meal was taken ale was drawn,
And talk and blood grew loud and warm.
When Rueben called in voice so slurred
For playing cards - unholy word.
Old Hugh bleached white and stood quite near.
"Take heed my son. Not that in here,
Remember thou the sabbath day."
At that they laughed - Hugh went away.

The pack of sin was cut unbound,
But six made incomplete the round,
Each pair of eyes turned to that man
Who had from sin so often ran.
"Make up the side", said Aaron then.
"Take that odd chair", he called again.
The old man choked with shame and fear
"The evil luck you'll bring me here".
Their mother pale with pious pride
Her outraged thoughts could scarcely hide.
With candle lit and muttering prayers
She sadly made her way upstairs.
Now all alone Hugh faced each son
An hardened eye o'er each did run.
He knew to late 'twas to chastise,
For wild the look was in their eyes.
Without removing boots or gear
He turned his back on sin and beer,
And loud his footfalls marked each stride,
The darkened stair his tears did hide.
Inside the bedroom furnished there
With bed and dresser, for each a chair,
High wife lay propped with pillowed down,
Her silver hair unbunned, hung down.
She looked expectant at his face,
He shook his head and found his place.
"Pass me the Book my husband dear,
At least the Word's not broken here.
We'll read a chapter, 'twill be best,
And let the devil take the rest."

Hugh sat him down upon the bed
And down his cheeks the salt tears shed,
Each found a crease upon his face
And like the thaw did downward race.
Then up he stood his passion gone,
Undressed and night attire pulled on.
"Goodwife", said he in voice so sad
"Read out the tale of the prodigal lad."
She found the gospel tale and read
Until the candle-light went dead.
Then age and sleep both right and just
Claimed their reward with simple trust.

While out the wind rose high and loud,
And whirled the mists like ghostly shroud,
And man and wife so fretful lay
As fitful dreams held them in sway.
Each faithless crevice found the wind
And curtains danced beneath the blind.
Somewhere outside a shippon gate
Did slam and slam without abate.
A hunting owl screeched loud with fear
And left the barn it loved so dear.
The embered wood inside the fire
Sprang up with life and roared with ire.
The six still sat and caroused there

And each in turn looked at the chair.
Some fate hypnotic turned their eyes
Tho' now too late for being wise.
The brew was strong, the cheese was old,
Each thought uncloistered left its fold.

When suddenly by the doorway there
They saw the one for the vacant chair.
The room fair reeked with brimstone smell
That clothed the stranger straight from hell.
"I heard you call me from outside,"
Said he with arms and hands held wide.
"A bite, a cup is all I need,
Then I will leave you, friends in deed."
"Pray take a chair," big William bawled.
"Say where ye from and what ye're called?"
"I've travelled far this week and more,
I'm Nick" he said, and crossed the floor.

His broad black cap hid well his face
As down he sat in the proferred place.
His skin was brown his hands were long
His teeth were pointed white and strong.
His eyes like coals flashed low and high
Like burning stars that cross the sky.
His cloak hung round him black and coiled,
The floor it swept yet 'twas unsoiled.
Moustaches fine, each end a hook
Gave him a devilish handsome look.
As book-learned Isaac drank his beer
He thought of the painted "Cavalier".

The devil ate and drank with stealth
And ne'er enjoined a toast to health.
On the mantle-shelf above the grate
His coal-black eyes bestowed their hate.
"What ails ye, friend?" said William pained,
When Nick his new-filled mug had drained.
The devilish face twitched mad with rage
And his finger clawed to the mantle-stage.
Six pairs of eyes both red and blear,
Turned to that spot which caused such fear.
"Pray clear that shelf," he spoke with dread,
"Or here and now I'll drop you dead."
"There's naught on here to cause you harm,"

Laughed Aaron as he moved the charm,
'Tis but a simple churchman's text
At which but Satan could be vexed.
But if it cause you pain or fright
I'll move it far beyond your sight".
At this his hand swept clean the board
And much refreshed the firegrate roared.
This seemed to please the devil then
And loud his laughter filled that den.

But still outside the night did glower
Great evil was abroad that hour.
The shippon gate still clanged its song
And kine enchained lowed loud and long,
For each now smelled the brimstone fire
And strained for freedom from the byre.
Old Hugh awoke from troubled sleep
And to the lattice-pane did creep.
He saw the chaos in the yard
And heard the bellowing, fearful hard.
He also heard the drunken roar
That came up from the bedroom floor.
He quietly dressed and found each stair
And saw a crack in the doorway there.
What sight revealed caused him to gasp
And quick his hand his mouth did clasp,
For there he saw them playing hard,
When John, the youngest dropped a card.
It fell between the strangers feet
(Like Pan's they were complete with cleat)

As quick as John, like he'd been stung
Betwixt the two lithe Enos sprung.
'Fore either one retrieved the card
Nick stood upright - stepped back a yard.
The sight they saw transfixed with dread
His cloak stood open bare his head.
Instead of shoes one for each foot,
He had two hooves and tail to boot.
His evil forehead dark, was horned,
A fearsome sight for all he formed.
"This night" he said, "You come with me
To dwell in hell for Eternity."

The stairfoot door burst open then
Old Hugh stepped out and faced the men.
"Now cross yourselves my children all".
At this the devil touched the wall.
The door flung wide and brimstone reek
Matched well the colour of each cheek.
Then he was gone 'fore holy zeal
As each repenting son did kneel.
And when 'twas o'er Hugh swept the board
And once again the firegrate roared.

Meanwhile the goodwife came downstairs,
And saw her kneeling sons at prayers.
Their tearstained faces were upturned
Each windowed heart showed true light burned.
Each swore an oath unto the Lord
That painted cards they now abhorred.
And Hugh smiled at each crimson face
So pleased that Good found Evil's place.

E'er after that, so the story goes,
Hugh Walker's sons were Satan's foes,
And as each sabbath came around
Unto the church they all were bound.
They even took the parson's place
When that good man found heavenly grace.
Their teams were loaned - from ties were freed,
They succoured all they found in need.
But strange to say they never wed,
Nor did they know a sinful bed.

While yet their sons were in their prime
Old Hugh and wife fell prey to time.
Their cortege down the lane was strung
Behind the hearse, three furrows long.
Yet not a mourner came inside
But took their seedcake there outside.
And in between the ale and wine
Some tipsy women kin did pine,
As stalwart shoulders bore the man
Before whose goodness Satan ran.

Now many years have passed away
Since Walker's brood found mortal clay.
Their croft is but a stony mound
O'ergrown with green where rabbits ground.
But their tale lives on and others tell
How near they came to Nick and hell.
A warning they to all blackguards
Who tempt the devil, by playing cards.

THE GERMAN BATTLESHIP "ADMIRAL SCHEER" ATTACKS AND SINKS THE ARMED MERCHANTMAN 'JERVIS BAY', ESCORTING CONVOY H.X.84 FROM HALIFAX TO ENGLAND. 5.11.40.

Out on the grey Atlantic swell
The convoy rolled from bell to bell.
Eight days out where the icebergs wait
In the murky mists of the Arctic gate.
Their speed eight knots by the slower ships,
Their funnels grey numbered thirty-six.
Each captain knew their chance was slim
'Gainst the Hunnish wolves and their packs so grim.

The watchers watched with eyes so red,
Off-watch they slept with unsleeping head.
Well they knew of their hapless state
Out there on the swell of the Arctic gate.
Unarmed except for the Jervis Bay
That patrolled on the flanks where the danger lay.
And she an old merchantman turned to force
With her puny guns and her mast for morse.

The morning and noon had come and gone
And the afternoon watch wore wearying on,
When alarm bells rang and the crew stood-to,
And the Jervis Bay brought her guns to view.
Far off there was seen on the Atlantic's grey waste
A much greyer form that moved with great haste.
The pride of the fleet of the Hun moved out there,
A battleship known as the Admiral Scheer.

She spotted the convoy so helpless and slow
And the old Jervis Bay out on the port bow
And full-throated her guns sang red loud and clear,
Eleven-inch and many had the great Admiral Scheer.
No gunner could miss the old Jervis Bay
As she turned to do battle and moved out to the fray.
She signalled aloft for the convoy to scatter
As the shrapnel cascaded her decks with a clatter.

Outgunned and out distanced she still tried to close
And the fire raked her side and her deck timbers glowed.
Her gunners were mangled but still she charged on
And Fogerty Fegen her captain was gone,
But obeying his last order to draw all the fire
She still charged the Hun but her plight was now dire.
The great Admiral Scheer still sang out hot death
And the old Jervis Bay gave vent her last breath.

The Hun crew stood watching as she sailed to her doom,
Her guns yet still firing though she was a tomb;
And the proud captain Kranke of the Admiral Scheer
Felt no pang of joy nor could his victory cheer,
For he knew that his battleship had nought won that day
When she fought the armed merchantman, the old Jervis Bay.
And he praised the old ship and her fine dauntless crew -
As she went down in glory - her ensign still flew.

And the convoy was saved from the Admiral Scheer's guns
Out there on the waste of the wild sea-way runs.
And Fogerty Fegen and his brave crew that died
Take their place on the roll that is their country's pride.
And rank in esteem with those others brave and true
Who made England's name when the Don hove to view
With the might Armada, the Spanish king's pride,
That ruled o'er the oceans so far and so wide.

But the old sea-dog captains, Lord Howard and Drake,
Sailed out to engage them, that great power to break;
And 'fore that day had ended no navy had Spain
By the good grace of God they were sank in the main,
And some that escaped fled o'er the board sea
And England's brave sons kept their loved country free.
Their names become legend in the history of war
And those who come after mind the brave ones before.

Like bold Richard Grenville who fought fifty three
With his little "Revenge" on the calm summer sea,
Near the tiny Azores so bejewelled and bright
Whose dawn saw the battle and the end of the fight.
Alongside these great then is Captain Fegen and crew
Who sailed to their deaths, so gallant, so true.
Old England will long tell with pride of that day
When the great Admiral Scheer fought the old Jervis Bay.

LONGNOR FAIR

When sweet September finds her crown
Her Thursday first knows wide renown.
'Tis then they wend their happy way
To Longnor races - there to play.

The tents their symbols gaily fly
And brightly tint the autumn sky.
And horses whinnying by the pound
As cheerful chattering goes around.
There some take Madame's sage advice
Before they play the darts or dice.
A silver coin across her palm
Will keep their hard-earned cash from harm.

The wily trickster's watchful eye
Marks well the fools as they pass by.
His oily tongue harangues the crowd,
His challenge casts in words so loud.
When out they trot into the field
Each price and bet is quickly reeled.

The flag goes down and they're away,
They cheer the dun and then the grey,
And thundering hooves ring out their song
'Twixt breathless pauses of the throng.
Round, round they go for one full league
Till horse and man show great fatigue.
Then down the straight and on to home
As flying steel casts flying loam.

Subdued but restless some now turn
To slake the fires that inward burn
With brimming tankards passed around,
And bread and meat with parsley's bound.
The day momentous nears its close,
In one's and two's each party goes.
Some ride some walk their homeward way
With hearts as light as they are gay.

FLATTERY

Of all the faults afflicting man -
And he's afflicted sorely -
A flattering tongue I number one
And that I say for surely.

23

THE LAMENT OF OWD NICK AND DEATH

When summer filled a happy day
And trees and meadows all were gay,
My steps as lightly found their way
To Stanley Moor,
Towards the inn there they would stray
Like as before.

Refreshed I sallied forth again
And reached the tree-lined, beechy lane,
Turned left about towards home again,
When from a wall
I heard two voices loud and plain,
My first name call.

I saw two men were sitting there,
One held a scythe had long grey hair,
His grizzled beard made up a pair,
It swept his breast,
"You've chose a day that's warm and fair
Whate'er your quest."

His crony then I saw full face,
My vital organ beat apace,
Owd Nick sat there in all his grace
And horn'ed glory,
"We're here to cull the human race",
He said with fury.

"We're sent to earth to do our duty,
The harvest falls when ripe and fruity,
Sometimes its my beholden duty
To gather greener,"
Nick then said, "Anyone's my booty
Both aged - and weaner, -

But there's this doctor chap I'll speak on
Who wields his bag around at Norton,   *Dr. F. McNellis*
Sometimes he visits rheumy Endon   *a friend of the*
When things look tragic;   *author.*
And when some patient deigns to hold on
He works his magic.

He comes from somewhere o'er the sea,
A place not known, spelt E.I.R.E.,
A genius chap we must agree
At healings art,
But how can Time and Death foresee
To play their part?

We both sit near with patience waiting,
While breath in body's fast abating,
When, wow! he enters orders stating,
This Cos physician,
Finds remedies, upsets our dating,
This learned magician.

He mixes poultices and lotions
With stuff from foreign lands and oceans,
And so that none can steal his notions
He writes in Erse,
With hierioglyphic marks and motions
That chemists curse.

The rate he's going no-one will die,
There'll be none for heaven and none to fry,
And Someone else will wonder why
There's no recruiting,
When earth should both homes satisfy
From flower to fruiting.

Nor are we 'lone in our sad grieving,
The undertakers call it thieving
When that man's magic art is weaving
To our distraction,
So much redundancy achieving
By one small faction.

Just hark to this, I mind it well,
(Said he whose kingdom's known as hell)
I'd marked a victim for mysel'
His name's no matter,
I'd laid a trap and cast a spell
With my best patter.

Out hunting went the one I'd take,
I hid behind a low fence brake,
I knew that way he'd surely make
(He tailed the field)
He'd sure be mine - his neck I'd break
Where it's never healed.

Up came his mare to take a look,
She leapt to clear the tiny brook
And would have done, but for my hook
That caught her leg,
Headfirst her rider fell to crook
And break neck's peg.

The joy I felt can ne'er be told,
Like finding rainbow's end and gold,
Another one to join my fold
I thought with pride.
I'll not be anxious, overbold,
Until he's died.

When curses! up another came,
He called the horseless rider's name,
He called to others of his train
"An M.D. quick!"
I fear our friend has proved fair game
For some black trick."

Well hidden from all mortal sight
And anxious for my prize by right,
I saw a figure that caused me fright
Come round the corner.
A starving undertaker's wight
Or early mourner? -

Ah! No! 'twas himself, the one we dread
Who knelt beside the rider's bed,
And like a priest that gives out bread
Began his saving,
With splints and cloth he bound his head
Against my craving.

To cut my story short I'll say
Inside six months - but for a day,
The man was well, robust and gay,
Had lost his fearing,
Come on, old friend, let us away
To find some shearing."

With that the two got to their feet
And arm in arm went down the street,
Owd Nick and Time accept defeat
I thought astonished,
So must we all our masters meet
To be admonished.

PROGRESS

The engines roar and wreak their doom
And cut and carve sweet nature's womb,
To widen roads and spread the towns
By grasping green to bloat their bounds.
With sickening thud the stately pine
Whose boughs once sheltered love divine
Falls to earth and leaves the space
Required for hurtling death's dark place.

'Tis sad to see the sward so green
Diminish, vanish from the scene,
As each day Progress sounds the knell
And some new plot falls to its spell.
Where in England can be found
A Hampden who will stand his ground?
Disdainfully spurn the golden palm
That stalwart souls so easily charm,
Who loves the land for what it is
And not for what is mine - or his.
Who loves 'this green and pleasant land'
And feels the joy few understand,
Who's grateful eyes can see the charm
That's found in wood and field and farm.

Is England's destiny to be
Enclosed by walls, or green and free?
Can she successfully withstand
And fight the trade of a greater land?
Or will she trying find the grave
And having lost have naught to save?
For as her struggles now appear
She's sacrificing all that's dear;
For every ten that knew the plough
There's scarely one that knows it now.

The simple joys and leisured art
(Each village craft then played its part)
Have long been swept by wealth away
Their night has come to end the day.
Each humble pleasure neglected dies
And ne'er again will ever rise.
The tinkling bells on brassy leather
The gaudy ribbons the proud ones tether
Upon each flowing mane and tail
To honour May, they never fail.
The maidens tripping round the stem
How sweet the countryside was then.
No more alas! are these sights seen
Where Progress shows its hand so mean.

The humble folk in tiny bowers
Awake to see the looming towers,
Participate in factr'ys toil
Forget forever the bleeding soil.
When swallow homes from foreign clime
And seeks the barn of an earlier time
He surveys the scene and turns to go,
And pity feels for Man's great woe.

Equivocation, Greed and Pride
Disdaining sweep our pleas aside;
And there upon the smiling land
Is seen the work of Evil's hand.
In this sad day and age 'tis known
That all things wealth can easy own.
The science of industrial war
Is new to those of rustic lore,
They fall an easy prey to those
Who gloat when fact'try's boundary grows.
The future near will raise their cries
When all is known before their eyes,
And call us Traitors, Fools and Lies
Who sold the Green for merchandise.

WHEN I FIRST MET MY JEAN

The rowan with its verdant boughs
Was springing bright and green,
And throstles sang full-throated there
When I first met my Jean.

The rowan's blossoms hung in June
And bees were busy there
And birdlings chirped within the nest
When I first kissed my fair.

The rowanberries red and ripe
The happy songsters clear,
The harvest that for them brings joy
To me brings many a tear.

The love she gave has quickly gone,
Another heart she has trepanned;
Another slave for her would die
If she but whispered her command.

LINES . . . .

You're lovely to look at, Miss Smith, I agree,
With dresses so fine and in fashion,
But mind how you step with your charming Jimmy,
The fly finds the spider as dashing.

TO THE PRIMROSE

She blooms, whom nature doth acclaim
As herald to the wakening plain.
Whom Spring hath sent with promise fair
To start the year with colours rare.
Angel flower, thy modesty outstrips them all
As shily thou peep'st from thy lonely stall.

Hear the gladsome lark proclaim
To all with joy thy well-loved name.
And Pheobus fondly gazes down
Upon thy brilliant golden crown.
So daintily thy nodding flowers
Pendulum-like, mark Spring's first hours.

Intrepid traveller of the naked sward,
The first much-loved of Nature's ward,
How longingly I seek thy charm
When Winter's storms subside and calm
Each searching eye looks o'er the lea
To catch the Spring - presaged by thee.

And Lo! some early promised morn
Behold! thy shimmering gold is born.
All hearts uplifting welcome thee,
But none dear flowerlet more than me.
Though March rampages o'er the plain
His bellow sings - 'tis Spring again.

BERRISFORD DALE

Heavenly cup, sweet vale,
Where Dove wild wandering flows,
Along thy sheltered meads and cliffs
Where scented woodbine blows.

Where low the verdant boughs are hung
To sweep the waters clear,
And torrents leap defiantly
Up o'er the silvery weir.

Morning sounds, the lark,
The wheeling plover's cries,
The blushing blue kingfisher darts
The skimming swallow flies.

Yon stony pathways by the stream
The waters wash so clear,
And cooling draughts sweet nature sips
Without one wit of fear.

LINES . . . .
ON HEARING A ROBIN
SINGING ON CHRISTMAS DAY

Robin, singing in the tree,
Enough, your point is taken,
You drew a thorn it made you free,
We killed and are forsaken.

THOSE WINTRY MORNINGS

The snow hangs heavy on the tree
And all is cold and grey,
Me bed so warm still clings to me,
I feel I must obey.
Those wintry mornings bleak and bare,
Shall find no friend in me,
I see no reason why out there
Should this poor mortal be.
I like to hear the feathered choir
Rejoicing at the dawn,
When Phoebus comes like ball of fire
As night's black sting is drawn.
When summer time is here to stay
And days are full of cheer,
And even'ng zephyrs sweet with hay
Sing out that summer's here.
But while the ground is cold and hard
I'll shun the wintry gloom,
The blazing hearth shall find a guard
Where e'er I find a room.

ON BEING STUNG BY A WASP
NEWLY RESCUED FROM A
TANKARD OF ALE

Ungrateful wretch, to sting the hand that fed thee;
Thy venomed prick is sore,
From now take heed - before me flee,
Or I shall take thy gore.

CRIPPLE BEN

One harvest-home it was and late,
I staggered out from Matt's back gate,
We having fixed a future date
To meet ag'en,
When nature called and couldn't wait
By Stannahs Pen.

That gate was made for folk like me,
'Twas not to high nor yet to wee,
But gate and man were meant to be
Used by each other,
The topmost bars I gripped as tight
As new-made brother.

How long I stood I cannot tell,
I watched the moon light Annie's well,
The very spot I thought, where fell
Old Cripple Ben,
Where, Annie swore, 'cos of the smell
She'd draw n'gen.

The fields were lit as bright as day,
I smelled the smell of second hay,
And evening stocks did all outweigh
With sweet perfume,
The whitest rose that hung so gay
By Maggie's room.

My fuddled mind was clearing fast,
I watched the heavenly clouds sail past,
An owl nearby let rip a blast
That chilled my blood,
Then by my feet it spewed its cast
Right in the mud.

From then an air crept on the scene,
And fear replaced where trust had been,
A burning smell came o'er, unclean
Like brimstone rare,
I clutched the topmost bars so keen
I broke the pair.

As I stood there with grumbling head
And wishing I was safe abed,
A form I saw that long was dead
In Stannahs Pen,
It stood awhile, then to me led -
Old Crippled Ben.

I saw straight through him to the well
(The place that sent him down to hell)
When from the castle struck the bell,
First one, then two.
He reached the gate - I nearly fell
When he came through.

He seemed to look me in the eye,
I swallowed hard, my mouth was dry,
The smile I tried went all awry,
"How are ye, Ben?"
I thought to humour him I'd try,
"You're back ag'en."

His peg-leg clicked upon a stone
And then he spoke with mellow tone,
"I see Matt's had his harvest-home
By look o' you,
To think that but for broke neck's bone
I'd been there, too."

We reminisced at bit at that,
And talked of Hatty, Ned and Matt,
Then Ben reached over for his hat,
"I'll have to go,
The boss down there's a bloody twat -
And I should know."

"I've been on ovens since I died,
He does it cos' it hurts my pride,
I've no-one there to take my side -
'Xept a witch,
And she goes whoring on the side,
The lousy bitch."

"Some days," said Ben, "He's not so bad;
He calls me Ben, and mate, and lad,
He tells me troubles, makes me sad,
And when I cry,
He'll laugh until it drives me mad
And wish to fry."

"So take this warning, lad," said Ben,
Beware of harvest-homes ag'en,
Owd Nick is waiting in his den
For likes o' you,"
With that he turned to Stannahs Pen,
And eyed the view.

His finger clawed towards the well,
"That dev'lish trap sent me to hell,"
(I nearly said 'I mind it well'
But feared to speak)
"And there I lay right where I fell,
For nigh a week."

"Nobody asked, nobody knew
Just why I happened in the dew,
But all the tale I'll tell to you
Before I go,
But just a swig of barley brew
That's there, I know."

He reached my pocket in one stride,
The pint went down his gullet, wide,
His clack moved like a horse's stride -
With ne'er a flaw,
But then, owd Ben would never bide
Till he'd supped four.

His tale to me he did relate,
How he with Annie stayed too late.
Her man had reached the garden gate
As he escaped,
Nor did he stay to share the fate
Of her, half-draped.

He stumbled through the brassic' patch
As Rueden found the front door latch,
And o'er the wall he failed to catch
The bucket-roll,
Then down he went into the cratch
As black 's coal.

Now some may say 'twas justified
That he had for his folly died,
And yet you know, 'twas Annie cried
Beside his grave,
She should have been the wartime bride
Of Ben the brave.

An accident it was, they said,
As solemn all to churchyard led.
I'll never speak of Annie's bed,
Nor Cripple Ben,
Nor from a harvest home be led
Past Stannahs Pen.

THE DOUBLE HARVEST
OF THE CORN FIELD

The ripened ears wave in the breeze,
(Less profit tho', the greener frieze)
And in that granary safely there
Has homed a tired but grateful hare.

But now with fear he hears the sound
Of reaper squareing round and round,
As nearer comes that rattling blade
He presses farther in the maze.

His sancturary now a square bit corn
Where lone he stays with fear forlorn,
For all the rest unto their lot
Have succumbed to the gun and shot.

Their mangled forms lie row on row
Beside the weasel, stoat and crow,
And wily fox who left his lair,
Now upward looks with glassy stare.

He hops unto the stubbled edge
And sees the dogs 'neath shaded hedge
And men beside - inactive now
They take their bite and mop their brow.

But, what's that thudding sound so near?
'Tis but a heart resounding fear,
Silent now to the other edge
Where the field slopes down to the rocky ledge.

Gently now on his hind stands up,
'Twixt him and freedom a thick-legged pup
Playfully sporting with its tail
A break-out now could never fail.

He gathers himself for one great spring
And moves with the speed that fear can bring,
Twelve bounds that is all to the ditch and the wall,
And away out of sight 'fore he heard the first call.

O' what a relief to see thee away,
Mayhap we may meet on a happier day,
Without gun or dogs to tear out thy heart
But as friends to enjoin - and to friendlier, part.

TO THEE, DEATH

Great leveller of man and beast
Our tears to thee will mean a feast;
From Royal head to me, the least,
You garner in,
Be it saint or sinner, heathen, priest
You always win.

We strut about from day to day,
Some cheat, some thieve, some selfish play,
And when on final bed we lay
In mortal fear,
We pray some Power your hand may stay,
With mercy hear.

But given leave and ill-got gain
We quick forget the dying pain,
As man 'gainst man we strive again
In ghastly hate,
Thus link by link we forge the chain
That holds our fate.

I pray thee though, forbear with me
And move my time to more A.D.
But only if it seems to thee
Both fair and just;
For pleasures have come late to me -
I've earned my crust.

And should you, Death, grant me my wish,
I'll drink your health with every dish,
I'll bless your name when others hiss
Their hate and fear,
I'll show them that your name means bliss
To those held dear.

And hold your hand 'gainst some I know
Whom life has dealt a cruel blow,
From day to day their mis'ries grow
Through other's greed,
Make their tormentors prostrate low
With utmost speed.

SWALLOWS

The swallows are gathering, 'tis time to depart
And find the warm clime so dear to their heart,
And soon o'er the ocean, they wing on their way,
'Tis goodbye for a while, till far away May.

Where Africa shimmers in the heat of the sun,
The prize that is theirs at the end of their run.
Through the warm sultry air they streak like the wind,
In the myriads of insects, their larder they find.

Now summer is ending and autumn is nigh,
And the dark stormy clouds bespoil the blue sky;
But the flowers and the fruits have no rival it seems,
To compare and delight, like the autumnal scenes.

There is little to detract from the dull wintry gloom,
When the dark leaden skies case the earth like a tomb,
Except when the robin fills the air with his trill,
And the pale bleary sun climbs the top of the hill.

But when winter is past and spring says goodbye,
A from so familiar is seen in the sky,
And the door to the barn is left open for thee,
Dear swallow, so beloved of the summer, and me.

LOST ON MORRIDGE!

Loud and dreary blew the wind
Across the moorland bleak,
And ne'er a pathway could we find
To take us back to Leek.
We sheltered in a rocky glen
That hid a tiny brook,
And jumped with fear so plainly when
An hare leapt from his nook.
A flickering light so far away
Shone like the Evening Star,
And we set foot to find the way,
So near, and yet so far.

We topped a hillock bathed in mist,
Then dropped to sheltered ground,
And saw the ghostly will-o'-wisp
Flit o'er the marshy ground.
The endless miles passed under foot
And we were sore indeed,
Once close we came to nesting coot
It cleft the air with speed.
And as we found a heather bed
Beneath a looming crag
We saw a sheep - 'twas long since dead
Near the antlers of a stag.
And lower down near a stumpy tree,
That lived I know not how,
We found the bones of a wallaby
Beside those of a cow.
We scarce could rest in that graveyard
So high up on the moors,
Where craggy hills kept watch and ward
Above the valley floors.

The dawn's first light fell on the dew
So silv'ry on the ground,
It woke the lonely brown curlew
Who billed his eerie sound.
And singing dawn with joyful glow
Bade all be calm and still,
As we stumbled on a cock's shrill crow
Was heard beyond a hill.
New life we found, we hastened on
To trace that homely call,
And there, behold! where lamp still shone
Stood a lowly cotters hall.

'Twas like the gates of heaven to those
Who'd passed a lonely night,
And we knocked the door until they rose
And gave us drink and bite.
Refreshed we left and soon were home,
For long we ne'er did stray
Beyond the sight of spire and dome
When night had closed the day.
Nor will we ere forget the time
When we went on that round,
And saw the sun twice heavenly climb
The tops of Morridge Mound.

O SPARE ME

Lord, hear thy humble servant's prayer,
"I'll stand mankind's derision.
But O, I'll lay my heart out bare,
Pray save me from religion."

REUBEN

When years shall give me yea or nay
To be at church each bright Sunday
I'll be inclined then to abstain
And never go there e'er again.

The reason Lord, for my evil thought,
Is the ill-luck each week's Sabbath's brought,
All pews are ta'en 'fore I arrive -
'Xcept one - and 'gainst that do I strive.

It is the one well-backed and bit
By those who 'fore me there did sit
But no objection do I raise
To follow those who sing Thy praise.

But kneeling there do I abhor
The fulsome figure there before.
His well-filled shiny trousers gleam
When caught by sunlight's darting beam.

When Rueben kneels to say his Grace
His rear's presented to my face.
'Twould make old Etna pale and wan
To hear the sounds that come therefrom.

And I defenceless murmer a text
That would the reverend greatly vex,
Could any christian praise Thee, Lord,
When Reuben frees what he has stored?

REJECTED LOVE

I pray thee cease thy warblings
Gay songster in the tree,
And pause a moment just to hear
A sadful tale from me.

Thy mate sits snugly in her nest
Her heart is full - o'erflowing,
She hears thy joyful loving lays,
Thy pleasures artless showing.

But what of me - in misery's bond,
Rejected by my lover;
O list to me thou woodland beau
Whilst I my heart uncover.

She flaunted well her plumage gay
To heaven I ascended,
Her eyes bewitched - O serpent thou -
Into the web I wended.

For days my heart's as blythe as thine
No gayer mortal living,
Now she has cast aside my love
Ungraceful, unforgiving.

So make thy song a dirge for me
For here no more I'll wander,
Lest mem'ries bitter bring their gall,
Tho' time may make them fonder.

Sing on dear birdling now I've done,
Pour out thy love - no measure,
But heed the words this mortal speaks
While winging on your pleasure.

AFTERNOON TEA AT THE VICARAGE

It befell one day ere Spring had flown
(The time when love's to Passion prone)
That tea was taken with the priest -
The goodly man gave such a feast -
There was ham he'd begged from yokel-farmer
Whose wife thought Satan could not harm her,
Cream and strawberries for the table
From those whose lives were so unstable,
Cakes from widows aged and poor
Who thought that Heaven for them was sure,
The landlord rich made his eyes shine
When he presented him with wine.
And so they passed the afternoon
To eat and sip and hymns to croon.

But a worried look was on the face
Of host and hostess in that place.
The woman of that bless'ed house
Was far from being big and stout,
And the dress she wore caused consternation
The vicar thought it a damnation.
Without support it sure would fall
(A secret prayer he oft would call)
But she flitted here and she flitted there,
And no one heeded the vicar's prayer.
Then when a song to Heaven was sent
He noticed quick a side long rent,
The dress was slipping from her back
And wide and wider grew the crack.

Quicker then he mustered words
"To the window all to see the birds".
His flock then did as he had bid
(While down her back the garment slid)
They gazed intently at the lawn
And all his friendships then were shorn,
For there, in throes of violent love,
Was Pip the mongrel and his dove.

MISTS OF MORNING

Wing me o'er the mists of morning
Where the Dove so gently flows,
Where the primrose shines at dawning
Where the woodbine softly blows.

Golden rays of sunlight gleaming
Hastes the mists across the fells,
Warms the landscape smiling beaming,
Day its richest promise tells

Wakes the larkling and the plover,
Eddies form on stilly pools
As the early preening rover
Mirrored there his ardour cools.

Wing me o'er the mists of morning,
Soon the lark will rise above,
Soon will rosebuds ope' adorning
Near the vale where flows the Dove.

BEING AN ADDRESS TO THE
CITY OF STOKE ON TRENT
UPON ITS JUBILEE

Salute to thee who wears the crowns!
That once belonged to six fair towns.
Example to the world thou'st shown,
How six made one that all could own.
And governed ably, right and fair,
Brittania's seals set firmly there.

Renowned thy name far o'er the seas,
Thy works pour out for all to please.
The mine and fact'ry, hid by smoke,
Marks well thy place in England, Stoke.
And now all hearts are gay and free,
On this, thy golden Jubilee.

Although no stately mounds are seen
To realize an artist's dream,
Thy beauty lies within the souls
Of those who fashion pots, and bowls.
Who, there within thy dimly walls
Create an art that all enthrals.

Sweet Trent so gay and blithely free,
A crystal stream ere it meets thee,
To later leave so black and sour,
Regretfully, its darkest hour.
The industries thy towns have made,
Have sullied her with all their trade.

Yet, proud am I, dear Stoke-on-Trent,
To own thee as a fond parent,
In thy grey streets and smoky towns
Are generous hearts that know no bounds,
Who'll drink a toast and say with me,
God Bless thee! on thy Jubilee!

THE VILLAGE

The morning sun its golden rain
With warming splendour greets the plain.
And chanticleer with lusty call
Proclaims day's vict'ry o'er night's pall.
The sleepy village stirs to life,
Each cot resounds the busy wife
As crackling logs burn in the grate
With hazy smoke a 'pluming straight.
The clanging milk-pail in the yard
And harsher sound of ploughman-bard
As raucously he tunes his song
To the milkmaid's lay, the herd among.
A tuneful chink of harness link
As noble one takes morning drink;
A fetlock deep wades in the pool
Before he takes his draughts so cool.
His ponderous strength so gently borne,
Prepares the field for autumn's corn,
As heavy ploughshare bursts the soil
His strength finds joy in honest toil.

The church, set in the little hill,
O'erlooks the village and the rill.
Beside the churchyard trim and shorn
There lies the school with daisied lawn.
From one the tuneful hymns of praise
Remind man of his stinted days;
Ere long the nodding elms will see
His final bourn beneath the tree.
The other with its youthful song,
Untuned and ringing out so strong.
No less sweet the tune to He
Who answered, "Suffer them to Me".
And He prayed that all would come as they
When all are called upon that day.

There to be judged not by their gain
Nor by their claim to titled fame,
But how they lived while yet on earth
And if they merit a christian's berth.
He also taught that wealth ne'er gave
A heavenly passage from the grave.

The even toll of hammered steel
That rings his trade with merry peal
Discloses to the curious eye
The blacksmith's forge in lane nearby.
Around his hearth of sparkling fire
The yarning group that words untire.
There yeoman tells the time-worn tale
Of better days ere crops did fail
And youthful ears take in each word
And wish those times could be returned.
Then silently they watch his skill
As iron bends to an iron will,
And shapes appear where none had been
As his brow reflects the firelight's gleam.
Then noble friend will stand aloof
At billowing smoke from upraised hoof.
Unflinching too when iron foot
Is noisy doused in steaming trough.
Then later proud with blackened feet
His ringing strides the lane will greet.

The golden orb rides on above
As the milkmaid ends her songs of love.
The cottage table scrubbed so clean
With humble fare is welcome seen.
The evening's sun now starts to wane
Casts lengthening shadows o'er the plain,
The ploughman from the field returns
There homely lamp and fireside burns.

The twilight air now falling cools
With icy fingers the misty pools,
While curtained light from windows shed
Ere long the village is abed.
The starry light lends to the scene
A glimmering peace, a joy serene.
While from the tavern murmering low,
The lated travellers homeward go.
Soon all is silent as the grave -
Except where watchdog sentinel bays -
Nocturnal wings take to their flight
And claim their kingdom of the night.

THE TRAVELLER'S REST
STANLEY

I've heard folk speak an adage true
"The Lord first takes the best."
Our prayers therefore must first begin
"Oh! spare the Traveller's Rest".
For tho' we're priv'lidged to enjoy
A merry heart and mind
Our earnest thoughts must think on those
Who follow on behind.
Who find a world of gloom and fear
And taverns dim and sour,
If we but save this friendly inn
'Twill be our finest hour.
And yeomen's sons - and their sons too
Like birds will come to rest
Where ale is good and friendship's true,
Inside the Traveller's Rest.

LINES .... ON RECEIVING A RHODODENDRON BUSH FROM (THE LATE) UNCLE GEORGE'S FRONT GARDEN AT STANLEY VILLAGE.

Now many years have flown away
Since first your crown rose from the clay,
And he whom we have mourned was here
To tend and guide you - upward steer.
And when establishment was fine
With joy and pride his face did shine.
How your fair blooms all else outshone
And stayed till June had come and gone.
The strangers passing Stanley Road
Would stay to see your crimson load.
Some leaned to touch your flowery stem,
Some filched from you a blood-red gem.
But Time and Tide man cannot stay
Your gardener's gone, his cot's away.
It's fell to me a task of pride
To take you home with me to bide.
A shady spot for you I've found
Where rowans grow o'er bowery mound,
And while for you I'll ply my skill
I know old George will nurse you still.

Stanley village. Showing the Traveller's Rest and next door below, Uncle George's cottage. A youthful Arthur Nash goes about his daily tasks.

LINES . . . .

And after toil we'll pleasures find
With barley brew and Bacchus,
Hell must be full or Nick is blind,
For —— still is with us.

53

BY STANLEY WAY

I wandered o'er by Endon way
And took the eastern lane,
At scenes so fond I'd pause and look,
Ere moving on again.
My steps were listless as if toil
Had robbed them of their spring,
When on the air sweet voices came
They had a laughing ring.

That way I bent my weary step
Which grew to eager stride,
I topped the brow, in Stanley went
Where door were open wide.
And laughing children sported there
Within fond parents gaze,
And somewhere near a maiden sang
In soft and loving lays.

The sight serene, the rural charm,
The maid - each child at play,
Aroused emotions in my heart -
A strong desire to stay.
A manly voice assailed my ear
And words and music told
Of love's young dream and parting bliss,
My steps I scarce could hold.

A country tavern I espied
Whence came and sound of fun,
It seemed the local folk here met
When toiling day had done.
A fitting sign o'erlooked the front
In gold and crimson dressed,
Informing all who passed that way
That here the "Travellers Rest".

Beside the door a rose-tree grew
With blossoms on its bough,
The music came from there - within,
With many voices now.
Just then it opened wide and clear,
A smiling face saw mine,
'Pray step inside good sir," she said,
'And taste our ale and wine."
'Tis balm unto the troubled heart,'
The comely matron said,
'The cares of this sad troubled world
Will leave you ere your bed."

I asked her name and where she dwelt,
If Stanley gave her birth,
'Pray no!" she said, "The world's my place,
'My friends they call me 'MIRTH'.

AND IS IT YOU, LASS?

And is it you, lass, and is it you
That sings so gaily in the tree?
'Tis not your love, a voice replies,
'Tis I, the mavis in the tree.

And is it you, lass, and is it you
That sings so gaily in the glen?
'Tis not your love the merle trills out,
But I will sing her song again.

HAPPINESS

Tis not from wealth I choose my home -
I live where laughing children roam.
My music is their tiny feet
That scramble o'er the floors and street.
Where boys are whooping merrily
And girls are singing cheerily.
Where parents clasp their infant child
With faces loving calm and mild.
Who know the joys of hearth and home
And have no wish to strive or roam,
Or seize the falsely glittery star
That tempts an erring foot afar.

I follow where sweet lovers stray
When sunset marks the closing day.
And where they wander through the grove
I lift their hearts with tender love.
Now mark the pattern of the dawn -
The blushing spring the budding thorn.
The tender daisies petals white
That shine among the grass so bright.
The cheerful song of birds at day,
The blushing rose the scented may.
When all these things are seen and heard,
Then what is felt is what I've stirred.

LETTER TO JOHN SALES, Esq., J.P. LEEK.

To you dear Sir I pen this line
(You will excuse my weakly rhyme)
With hope it finds you well and fine,
And hale and hearty,
And still dispensing words like wine
So crisp and tarty.

A victory yours - the last election,
A public nod for your perfection,
Some part has needed your protection
And honest zeal,
They know it would have your correction
For their own weal.

In council work you never tire,
Their lethargy you seem to fire,
With resonant voice that marks your shire
You chivvy on,
Then stop to help, advise, admire
What some have done.

As J.P. though some know you better
When stood arraigned for crime or debtor,
They know that justice without fetter
Will be their fate,
A hearing fair by book and letter
They stand and wait.

I hope the years will treat you well,
That you and yours will happy dwell,
And that for long you will excel
In council - J.P.
And at the end with Him to dwell
And reap your bounty.

FOR YOU, A ROSE

For you my love this rose I send
Blood-red and dripping wet with dew,
O to its message please attend,
Its speaks of love that's fair and true.

What mem'ries may a flower provoke?
What joy and gladness too?
I send to you this blood-red rose
To say my love is still for you.

The scented petals rare and fine,
My pulse's race so madly start;
The flowerlet lies in your white hand,
Its thorn lies buried in my heart.

O THE WEARY DAY

O, the weary day is spent and done,
The swelling moon is bright above,
The toil, the tasks, the harvest's won,
Now I'll away to meet my love.

To win her heart's my only goal,
Her favourite flowers have I to hand,
I'll promise all - my very soul,
And seal it with a golden band.

O Time, find sleep while I'm with her,
Or drag a weary foot so slow,
A day, a month or e'en a year,
From ages can be spared, I know.

HOSPITALITY

Mellowed sweet by mouldering years
Knowing joy and oftimes tears,
All alone on Endon height
Shining like a star at night,
Stands the lone Lawn Farm.

Look beyond the latticed pane
Of that farm atop Park Lane,
See inside there homely cheer,
Friend or stranger never fear,
Welcome to Lawn Farm.

Yeoman stock bred in those walls,
Honour, Friendship never palls,
And hospitality was born
In the farmhouse there called 'Lawn'
In Endon's old Park Lane.

So if dear stranger, you should find
Your steps have wandered never mind,
I'll guarantee you any cash
You'll welcome find with Arthur Nash
In Endon's old Lawn Farm.

THE TRAMP

Along the highways measured strolling
Jauntily without a care,
See him with his pack and doling
Hanging from his waistring there.

Cheered by summer's sun so warming,
Caring nought tho' should it rain.
Pitying the faces forming
At each passing window pane.

From his freedom ne'er will sever,
Come what may, but death will part;
Born to wander on for ever
Vagabond of lonely heart.

OVER THE MEADOW

Over the meadows and over the lea,
Where the bright waters flow there would I be;
Where the white swan glides away to her nest,
By the cool shady bank there I love best.

Where the bright fishes glide down in the reeds,
There the green mosses hang morn's dewy beads;
Low sweep the hazel boughs touching the streams,
There the cool waters sing, there let me dream -

Dreaming of love while the bird's singing clear
Dreaming of one whom I love, O so dear.
Sweet Dove - my own muse - bear my song to her ear,
O bid her draw nigh and remain ever near.

O ENVY NOT THE MAMMON SIGN

O envy not the man of wealth
With trappings fine to show,
His worries you may never see
His troubles never know.

For it is true and mark it well,
No man escapes with pleasures,
For sickness comes or other ills
To blight the gift of treasures.

Just take enough of worldly wealth
Put happiness 'fore all,
And envy not the glittering gem -
Its brightness tends to pall.

If further proof you need my friend,
What gave this thought its birth -
The Greatest, wisest One that lived
The poorest was - on earth.

LINES . . . .

The clouds ride high
Beyond the sky,
Like man's unquenched ambitions,
At other stars he casts his eye -
Those clouds are mere partitions.

LEEK

QUEEN OF THE MOORLANDS

Among the hills she has her lofty throne,
The fairest town this land has ever known,
Upon whose charms the sun seems ne'er to tire
For twice he lingering sets behind St. Edward's spire.
Her industries are light and fine, and rare.
Her market stands enclosed within a cobbled square.
Renowned her taverns for their homely cheeer,
Far-famed her Walk and Show each happy year.
See her in spring from where Morridge looks down,
See her in summer with flowers in her crown,
See her in autumntime, purple and gold,
See her when winter arrives, ermined and cold.

The tall white column rears its granite head,
And tablets at its feet there name her valiant dead;
With seats around for resting, talk and shade,
And on the east a garden for unseeing patrons made.
Her famous parks, well-tended, please the view
With English flowers arrayed - and rare ones too.
Well blest with halls of learning for her young,
Where pen and brush are skilful taught, and many a foreign tong
The local news, the deaths, all fetes and crimes,
Her citizens find all revealed inside the 'Post and Times'.

Nearby bright Churnet chatters o'er her stony ways,
And many an angled stem, so still, her water plays.
(Though some may take a longer step and early leave their berth
To sieze the splendid trout that lie in pools at Tittisworth)
As now she hastens on her way hard by some willowed boom
Where quivering aspens closely stand and cast their shady gloom.
Now see her bounding waters in full spate
As hurtling on she leaps the weir and passes Wallbridge Gate,
Or, thundering fresh from some torrential shower
She breaks her banks and spreads, a wanton in her power.

But yet o'er all in this fast following age,
There hangs a cloud so black, of boding ill-usage.
As witness other towns subdued by Mammon in this shire,
Where time-won beauty deathly gropes amid the darkening mire.
Where spoiling hands, destroying all, so anxious to erase,
May raise a hideous Gorgon there, and on it pour their praise.
And in their train an alien breed comes trampling o'er the green,
And rural arts and rural ways may never more be seen.
But in the name of Progress vague a heritage cast down;
May this ne'er be the fate of Leek, the dearest, fairest town.

ON PSALMS

He told them that a rich man's wealth
Could never brook the tide,
That gold to man was ever bane
If he wished heaven's side.

He pointed to the lily fair
In nature's splendour shown.
The greatest, wisest king on earth
Such beauty ne'er could own.

He told them of a widow poor
Who gave her mite to pray.
Much greater was that price to Him
Than what the richer pay.

And lastly drew to Him a child,
And took it on His knee.
And caution bade, if one hair be hurt
Those same would damned be.

THE DANDELION

Spurned from the green by the iron fork and spade
Uprooted by Man where his green lawn is laid,
Thy bright buttery-yellow condemned to the heap
Thou art labelled 'a weed' because thou art cheap.

Without cultivation or a welcoming hand
Thy head elevating thou surveyest the land,
Thy sweet golden fronds smile up at the sun
So perfect their shape like a chrysanthemum.

Then along comes dim Man to pierce thy sad heart,
Cut down in thy prime when thy beauty did start,
The white milky-sap pours from thy tap-root
And crushed thy end finding 'neath iron-shod boot!

THE SHOW

The rich man shows his lady fine
In cloaks and frailties dressed,
But of them all throughout this land
My Meg I love the best.

For wealth gives them a flippant heart
Cuckolding is their law,
And when they're seen out, arm in arm,
Just show is what it's for.

But my true love is true to me
And though her dress be plainer,
Her qualities, so fine and pure,
None living can contain her.

ILAM

How blest sweet Ilam to enfold
Such lovely rivers twain,
The gentle Dove and Manifold,
That join on thy green plain.
Where noble Hall 'midst leafy bower,
Keeps watch and ward so well,
And looks across from lofty tower
Where stone speaks those who fell.
The church and churchyard with its green
So crossed and hewn to form
So sad, and yet so gay it seems
When blossom decks the thorn.
The meadows with their winding lanes
That lead to fair Dovedale,
That sits 'twixt hills of lofty mien,
And lined with cloven trail.
Each little cot with garden neat
And flowers of every hue,
With changing scene each season greet
And brings delight anew.
Where roadway winds up steeply hill
The stony schoolhouse stands,
Where early bell the air will fill
And bring the scurrying bands.
There, Hazleton looks o'er the vale
From tree-topped height so grand,
And Druids' graves fill village tales,
And leaden mines the land.
How blest is Ilam with her store
Of nature's treasures rare,
May they remain for evermore
For all mankind to share.

ENDON

Fair Endon, where the tall trees touch the sky,
And splend'rous dawns o'er Stanley Moor illume the morning sky,
Where birdsong adds its tuneful lay as waking time is near,
And streams rush past their willowed banks, or stilly lie, so clear.
Where springtime calls to ply her art before she's elsewhere seen,
And meads are dressed in pearly dews to show where she has been.

Sweet Endon, in summer's languid day
And leafy lanes of arboured rest are filled with scented may,
Where chequering lights play through the leaves and touch each flowerlet th
And mantling ivy leaps the walls and leaves no stone to stare.
Where cooling mists on the quiet air hang low their silvery veil
And evening skies, long-lingering flee the darkening shadowy dale.

Quiet Endon, when whispering night is near,
And gentle breezes bear the sounds of village life so dear.
Where slow the brown-eyed, gentle herd, makes homeward ways alone,
And round the barn the gadwing flies his tuneless, endless drone.
Where soon the owl will leave his roost and fly an eerie round,
And timid feet so silent, flee towards the brown earth mound.

THE SOLEMN HILLS

The solemn hills uplift their timeless heads
As silent veils of chilly mists sweep by;
No creatures find or leave their earthly beds
As early morning fills the greying sky.

'Tis 'neath this world that mortal things are found
Where life surrounds each wood and pasture green,
The lark mounts high to lay his morning sound
And sunlight gilds with gold the rippling stream.

Here joy and love and sorrow grows
And things that move and breathe,
But where cold winds the stormy hill-top blows
Those silent mists of silvery death enwreathe.

The kingly eagle soaring wheels to miss
Those craggy tops and dreary dark abyss.
The power that formed the Universe and sky
It seems that spot neglected - left to die.

No furry form for food goes whimpering by,
No feathered nestling tempts the widening sky;
Nor yet has human voice e'er filled the air -
Nought but the sorrowing winds find solace there.

O' SIX WEEKS A'COURTIN'

O' six weeks a'courtin' and nothing to show,
I'm six weeks a'courtin' and nothing to show,
The trees have their blossoms hung out on the bough,
I've wooed and I've charmed her as best I know how.

The sweet budding roses now open to flower,
The minutes race by me to melt in the hour.
The time is not ripe and this much I agree,
The sweetest of fruits lie atop of the tree.

O' six weeks a'courtin' and nothing to show,
With some it takes longer's a fact that I know.
It could be I'm losing my grip as a beau -
O' six weeks a'courtin' and nothing to show.

AT CHRISTMAS TIME

At christmas time, at christmas time,
The fields are white with snow,
And busy people hasten on
And tradesmen come and go,
A magic 'something's' in the air
And shops are dressed for style
With mistletoe, and holly green,
And boxes, pile on pile.
And everyone says "How d'ye do?",
And smiles are all around.
And on the christmas tree bedecked,
Are presents, gaily bound.

The church and chapel with pious zeal
Present the Christmas tale,
And willing hands have made the Crib
Complete in all detail.
The Wise Men sit around the Babe,
The ox and donkey stare,
While Angels sing their carolled joy
For Him, asleep in there.
And this was how it all began
So many years ago,
Sweet Jesus Christ came down to earth
So man may goodness know.

FICKLE FORTUNE

I'm done with fickle fortune's trust
And her maidservant woman,
To wait on either brings man rust,
From now fate's wheel 'I be hummin'.

Of mine own ship I'll master be
The helm's turn be my choosing,
And will I sail so wildly free
And grumble not at loosing.

And grumble not at losing boys,
For what's this life but sailing,
Of sad goodbyes and fond ahoys!
Smooth waters - stormy boiling.

So off with fickle fortune's chain
And likewise maid alluring,
Death's hand awaits whate'er the train
Life's wants and wishes curing.

O' WHY?

Why is this life so hard
And why is Grief e'er nigh
Why's Pleasure shown a yard
And Toil shown twice as high
Why must I sweat and labour
Inside this tunnelled tomb
Without a friend or neighbour
Down in the earth's black womb.
Why did the good Lord make us
Each different from the rest,
Why do we round the rich ones fuss
Yet spurn the poorer guest.
O' God, I'm but a humble lad
And life to me seems queer,
I pray Thee spare me something glad,
Or take my soul from here.

ON A DEPARTED LOVE

O will I find you by the stream
Where skies in stilly pools are seen?
Or will you seek the cooling shade
The spreading chestnut's arms have made?

Maybe you'll wander o'er the hill
Where peaceful herds are lying still.
Or where the shepherd tends his flocks
While children gather ladysmocks.

Perhaps you've wandered o'er the green
Where oft we'd sit and love, and dream.
Where on the broad oak stem a part
We blazoned on a loving heart.

Or are you where the heaving turf
Is tablet-marked with name and birth?
And marbled round from head to toe
To mark your quiet cell below.

ON WOMAN

From long ago - since Time was young
A woman's weapon has been her tongue;
God took from her all Manly strength
But endowed her with a tongue of length.
He coupled this with biting Wit
'Gainst which 'tis vain for Man to pit.
The only thing mere Man can do
Is, from the Shrew to bid Adieu!

SAMMY SLADE

The world was once a doleful place
All frettin', tears and moaning',
And folk went on their daily round
With voices hoarse with groanin',
Owd Nick he rubbed his hands with glee
Mankind he had well-haltered,
But when the Lord took stock o' things
The situation altered.

The grey was swept from off the skies
And flowers grew all around;
And people smiled and talked so wise
And laughter was their sound,
Bacchus sent his wonderous cheer,
The Muses homage paid,
But greater far was Man's last gift -
When MIRTH sent SAMMY SLADE.

THE WINTERY WIND

The wint'ry wind blows wildly by,
The rooky clouds race o'er the sky,
The cattle shelter in the lea,
But there is nowhere left for me.

The woodland trees are bare and stark,
Coccoons lie snug behind the bark,
Around the stem the wind blows free,
And there is nowhere left for me.

The ivied wall though, halts its pace,
The moon serene enfolds her face,
A voice sincerely calls to me,
"But we have room enough for thee".

I peer across the mossy stone,
At each cold cross that stands alone,
"Pray be at rest, and pass my door,
My fellow creatures need me more."

PINK-E'E

I mind a time - now long ago
When to the corner shop we'd go,
And critic' gaze at all on show,
'Fore ha'p'ny spend.

Eyes so big would roam around,
And view with hungry looks the mound
Of luscious sweets and fruits well-bound
With tinsel show.

A grimy hand still clutched the coin
Ere Pink-e'e's hand would it purloin,
And throw it careless like to join
Its many brothers.

We wondered why a man of wealth
Should take our bit by business stealth,
When florid face betrayed his health
He'd never spend it.

We judged him grasping so was he,
At night we'd bang his door and flee
But if he caught us, 'cross his knee
He'd bend a buttock.

Complaining words nor dare we utter
He'd turn our folk into the gutter,
That man who sold his marg' for butter
Landlorded houses.

On summer nights when all sat out
And ate their chips and drank their stout,
From Pink-e'e's door would come a shout
And out he'd stagger.

His one good eye would glare around
He'd sway and swear but keep his ground,
As round his wrist the leather wound
Away we'd scatter.

I've seen him eat a whole crab raw
From mussel-man who brought his store
On handcart, that around he'd draw
Crying, "Muss-ee-lo!"

But nothing would he give to them
By whom he lived he'd see them clem',
His Nemesis has been the Crem',
Just retribution.

ON CRITICISM

Man can only see within his own vision,
And reason upon that which he sees -
For his own liking or displeasure.
He cannot reason for his brother,
Nor can he truthfully discriminate for all,
Since each mind is individually attuned
To a different plane. Therefore will it be seen
That all things on earth, and all things
Created by man, will find beauty and pleasure
In the eyes of some beholder.
So will each and all things be admired
In this wonderful, wonderful world.

STANLEY

O do some worthy pike and perch
Still bite in Stanley Pool,
And do the anglers on its banks
Still heed the golden rule?
Do swallows still choose Colley's farm
To build their clayey nest?
And is the rose tree by the door
Outside the "Travellers Rest?"
Say, is mine host there still named Mould,
(My fancy now takes flight)
And do the brasses hurt your eyes
Because they're shining bright?
Is that old clock still hanging there
All varnished, clean and proud,
And does it stroke the half and full
With jarring notes so loud?
Do fires still blaze inside the grate
No matter what the time?
And is the entry black and white
From cleaning tar and lime?
Does Uncle George still use two hands
To drink his cup of stout?
Does Harold's face go long and grim
When 'Time' is shouted out?
Is Ernest still a man of words?
Does Jess still sport a gun?
Do they still wrangle at the bar
When work is o'er and done?
And is that tavern still the spot
Where care his leave he takes?
And do the happy throng still meet
To share in Stanley Wakes?

MANIFOLD - PLEADS FOR LIFE

ON PROPOSED FLOODING OF
MANIFOLD VALLEY TO
MAKE A RESERVOIR

I rise with Dove near Three Shires Head
(And near to Ilam are we wed)
Then hastening down the mountainside
I wander through green meadows wide.
The centuries have marked my way,
I've worn through sandstone, granite, clay.
I chose this valley for my own -
From infant stream to river grown.

I scorn the weirs along the way
Where laughing sportive children play,
The pensive anglers' stem I bend,
They love and treat me as a friend.
Those massive trees that shade my banks
I've known since they were spindleshanks.
The brids whose nests there gently sway
Have nested there for many a day.

The well-worn paths that sheep have trod
Still lead to beauty made by God.
The poets often tread my ways,
And I inspire them and their lays.
There's one I know who finds my side
And hears the muses in my tide.
He sings my praises in his line
And paints my beauty, rare and fine. -

Now though it's vain that I should do,
I must agree with what is true.
For thousands come to see my art,
And walk my length from end to start.
I've heard some say, while passing by,
That Europe ne'er with me can vie.
While Yankees from the other side
Say things that make me blush with pride.

Some single folk beside me lay
And return in two's another day.
And many a time - till life will end
They come to see me as a friend.
I like to dream my valley floor
May bring their kind for evermore.
May lovers choose my rushing tide
Their whispered secret words to hide.

May thrush and blackbird fill the vale
With tuneful songs their ears assail.
May children rushing round with glee
Store up some memory fond - of me.
O' may I plead with you for life,
I've never caused one sturt nor strife.
Take heed you sons be not o'er-bold,
He'll damn himself, who dams Manifold.

LINES . . . .

Take heed when pointing a finger,
For the earth is round.

AT THE CHURCH

Old Nick fair beamed with heartfelt glee
As there he sat beneath the tree,
"So far the lot will come to me",
He cried and danced,
He slapped his thigh and then knee
As round he pranced.

With solemn looks the mournful throng
Thro' lych and churchyard passed along
And pointed where some friend had long
Been laid to rest,
(As just as quick they point the wrong
That's in the best)

They entered then the hallowed hall
Where many a text there on the wall
Prevailed on Man he should recall
His sinful state,
That on his knees repenting fall
'Fore it's too late.

Yon cot of stone beneath the hill
That's scarred and worn by nature's will
Yet from whose doorway welcomes spill
To passing neighbour,
To stop and chat, or taste a gill
When free from labour:-

In there where happiness abounds
Is seldom seen grim Care's dull frowns,
But often Want has worn his crowns
Tho' dignified,
Then left for other homes and bounds
Where folk abide.

From this bright cot the two set forth -
No better two e'er trod the earth -
Tho' Time, with thongs aged legs did girth
And breath was short,
But yet to sing and talk with mirth
Was what they sought.

They reached the churchyard (soon their bed)
And 'fore their goodness Satan fled,
The path they took when they were wed
Brought mem'ries dear,
And Maggie's cheek so wan went red
With happy tear.

With faltering steps they reached the door
(Inside all pews were ta'en before),
Both turned away with hearts full sore
For it was known,
That they put praise to God before
All things they own.

Before they reached the ivied porch
There shone a light like brightest torch,
E'en Pheobus' rays it did debauch
So bright it shone,
And Maggie, fearing they would scorch
Clutched tight to John.

They heard a voice speak loud and clear,
'Twould seem the lips were by their ear
"I see for you there's no room here",
And both did nod;
"Take heart, there's none for Me I fear,
And I am God."

SHE FLOWS CONTENTED

She flows contented on her way
Unsullied yet by man or clay,
Her song goes winging bright and gay
To shady bowers,
Where minstrels come to tune their lay
In lightful house.

How wanton leaps she o'er the ford
To send a foaming bubbling horde
Where speckled trout lie, stilly moored
By cooling banks,
The piscatorial art thou'st stored
With any ranks.

A'down yon lea where aspens wave,
Sweet Manifold awaits, thy slave;
I've heard them say in words so grave
There's none thy peer,
That Yankees o'er thy waters rave
When they are here.

And I, sweet Dove, thy rustic bard,
Oft find seclusion on thy sward,
Away from life - and critics hard -
I peaceful rest.
To me of rivers made by God,
Thou art the best.

BLESSINGS

Sixty seconds make a minute,
Be sure and pack each moment in it.
Sixty minutes make an hour,
Drive sweet joy with all your power
Four and twenty make a day
Smile, and care will never stay.
Seven days will make a week,
Let no tears stain your cheek.
A year embraces fifty - two -
To end, and start sweet joys anew.

Greet each new day with happy smiles
And troubles lose their many wiles.
The birds can sing and they've no wealth,
Grim care can ne'er catch them with stealth.
When next you hear the sweet birds sing,
And Cares and Woes their troubles bring,
Just whistle like the little bird
And armoured joy will your heart gird
Think on those blessings He's bestowed,
'Twill lighten e'en the heaviest load.

EPITAPH
ARTHUR BRENNAN
OAKHILL, STOKE

Formed in nature's noblest art,
Never yet a kinder heart,
Lord, his place is at Thy knee,
For here on earth he cherished Thee.

I LIKE

The smell of the tar when its poured on the road
'Fore the roller will crush and the earth will enfold.
The stable and shippon all whitewashed and cleaned
And the sweet milky-smell of a calf as its weaned.

A hedgerow in May when the blossom is out
And no zephyr disturbs all the scent they give out.
The stock that will open for eventide show
And during the darkness will soft perfume blow.

When midsummer comes to the woodland and fell
And bees find the vine where sweet honeysuckles dwell.
The grass and the thyme when bruised under foot,
And the turning of hay when the meadows are cut.

The odour so clean of the pine in the wood
And the scent of the rose newly opened from bud.
The white-clover field where the butterflies linger,
And mint when its broke - and also sweet-ginger.

The smell of the salve when applied for the rheum,
And the soil newly turned - and the elder in bloom.
The suit that when new just for Sunday is worn
When the children sing hymns on the vicarage lawn.

A fragrance may wake in the nostalgic mind
A memory of sadness or joy left behind.
Then heartfelt the thoughts o'er the years swiftly fly
And present and past by this union tie.

RUDYARD

ON PROPOSED FLOODING
OF RUDYARD VALLEY, TO
MAKE A RESERVOIR.

So fair thy vale where waters lie
And mirror clouds up in the sky.
Or maybe tossed in wild torment
They heave their waves in mad ferment.
Umbrageous banks thy pools adorn,
The chestnut, oak and flowering thorn,
All in their turn stand beauteous there
While eyes in worship stand and stare.

The crafty angler's match is found -
Your piscatorial arts abound -
From east and west, from north and south,
Your name's on every christian mouth.
Men stretch upon the cooling banks
And cast their lines of several hanks.
Not caring if a fish should take,
But more from labouring toil to break.

See there the happy family pass
To picnic on the verdant grass.
The shouting youngsters rushing by
To catch the elusive butterfly.
The smiling couple's hands entwined
Some far secluded arbour find,
And 'neath some shade to pledge a word,
Alike unseen, and yet unheard.
O God! 'mongst this, Your loveliest work,
Some blackguard sons of satan lurk.
They seek destruction and to drown
This precious gem in Stafford's crown.

A TENDER THOUGHT

A pitying felt for thee and thine,
Whose toil ne'er brings them ale nor wine,
That's why I let thee sip at mine,
And watch thy antic,
As round and round thou buzzest fine,
So gleeful, frantic.

Pray drink thy fill my buzzing friend,
Thy broken heart good ale will mend,
So happy then thy way to wend,
To hive of gloom,
A bit of joy by thee I send,
Into that tomb.

Where industry is all thy life,
And sluggards die by arse-hid knife,
Ungrateful Queenie - cruel wife!
Unhappy Drone!
Who rules as King when love is rife,
For one alone.

But after giving her thy all
They turn thee out from thy love-stall,
To face a death I dare'nt recall,
Because they're neuter,
And thou art blest above them all,
With shot and shooter.

I too must face a lashing tongue
When I return from bliss among.
And even dreamt that I've out slung
My Queen of Hearts,
E'er after that she's loving clung
To blissful arts.

So let us pledge each to the other -
Thou'st supped my ale, that makes thee brother -
That we'll endeavour to recover,
Man's greater state,
And keep the female as a lover,
'Fore it's too late.

THE RAG AND BONE MAN

"Rags and bones - Rags and bones"
He cries his happy song;
His little cart bumps o'er stones
As his pony trots along.

Balloons and goldfish, little toys
Shown gaily on his cart;
From the wide-eyed train of girls and boys
Excited clamours start.

Clothes and jumble piled up there
Betoken his reward,
While round his cart they stand and stare
At seemly worthless hoard.

The pony starts with light clip-clop,
As slowly on his way,
The 'Rag and bone man' takes his shop
Down other streets to stray.

His gnarled hand waves a fond farewell
To those whom he decoys;
And they wave back balloon or bell
And other gaudy toys.

THE COAL PICKERS

The pit-bank gleams with flitt'ring light
Like glow-worms on a summers night
As colliers traipse into the cage
That takes them down to gloomy maze.
Then wheels spin fast and coal is drawn
As earths black wealth is quickly shorn.

When daylight gilds the dirt-tip mound
Where self-lit fires so warm abound,
The wagon trains begin their toil -
To move the hard won earthly spoil.
The powerful shire's resounding tread
So measured, wakes the sleepy head,
And rumbling carts large steel-shod wheels
The trembling earth resenting feels.

Nuts and lumps, large beans and slack,
The noise, the smell, the whips that crack,
All fill the morning on the road
As all in line they draw their load.
On - on they trudge, mile after mile,
Each keeping true the snaking file;
The waggoners hold each giant head,
Each patient friend so easy led.

The granite sets give their approach
And waiting groups around encroach;
Small children, poor, clutch each a bag,
Tho' clothed themselves in poorer rag
Behind the carts they follow there
And bumpy sets spill them their share;
Each coal that falls upon the road
Tis theirs by right of law that's old.
Their fingers numb with clutching hard
Can hardly hold the crust of lard
That they partake between each train
As on they go, again, again.

Eyes for want of sleep are red,
Limbs are stiff for want of bed,
Pinched and drawn each face so wan,
Hope, so early came - was gone.
Each bit they pick up from the road
Their future speaks in black, black gold.
Ere tender years have quickly fled
Those mites to mines are eager fed.

The selfish tradesman looking on,
Sees one small hand reach up and on
And take a cobble - yet to fall,
Then, "Whip behind the cart", he'll call.
That leathered lash so long and coiled
Bites deep upon a hand that's soiled
And salty tears so quickly flow
And hands once numb begin to glow.

When last the wagons cease to roll
The groups disperse with hard-earned coal,
To face, maybe, a tyrant's rage
That little pickings ne'er assuage.
Both black and blue from hand and foot
To schoolhouse door ere it be shut,
To nurse their fear of further pain
When early morn wakes them again.

For them no joy of parents love,
Nor blessing yet comes from above,
Born by mischance, they quickly learn
Their lowly state all others spurn.
In some dark corner see them creep
And in their mis'ry silent weep.
Uncared, such wretchedness abounds
To blot brave England's fairest towns.

ON SEEING A GOLDFINCH
IN A CAGE

What cruel wretch ensnared thy wing
Did to this shameful prison bring -
To face a death that 's lingering -
Thy flutt'ring feather,
So his lone ear may hear thee sing
Some slavish measure.

A curse upon his heart of stone,
For this vile deed he'll ne'er atone
E'en yet, I'm sure he'll fret and moan
At 's sorrowful living,
His selfish act stands out alone -
Has no forgiving.

A'top some budding tree or vine,
Thy notes rang out with joy divine,
Intent upon thy lovers thyme
Hid there below,
She drew thee to the treach'rous lime
That laid thee low.

The morn will miss thy eager song,
Out there, not here, dost thou belong,
With all the rest of nature's throng
So happy living,
Thy voice with gladness clear and strong,
So joyful giving.

No chance to bid thy fond adieu
To hers and thine, and all thy crew,
To see thee fast doth sad imbue
This rustic heart,
That knows the evil pinions do
To thy free heart.

No misty tear conglubes thine e'e,
Tho' from thy stem thou'lt surely see
You feathered choir in the tree -
More freer neighbour, -
To whistle now I'm sure 'twill be
Thy greatest labour.

Fret not, dear birdling in thy cell,
That fearful heart a moment quell,
While I sincerely to thee tell
Of dimly Man,
Who's made this earth into a hell
Since he began.

The Master's Hand gave thee thy voice
To tell the world be glad, rejoice,
In this bright task thou art His choice,
So do not pall,
He hears e'en the sparrow's voice,
And notes its fall.

Why, he who snared thee for his own
Bright freedom ne'er himself hath known,
But 'neath his master's heel doth groan,
And beg his bread,
Yet he'll to Mercy be unknown
Until he's dead.

And so mankind in tearful state
With Want and Trouble at the gate,
Turns on each other Greed and Hate,
With hellish passion,
For Gold and Blood, insatiate,
Their fangs are gnashin'.

I'll never sleep for thought of thee,
See, now the door is wide and free,
I'll suffer what they do to me
To see thee winging,
And later in thy favourite tree,
I'll hear thee singing.

LETTER TO CHARLES C. CRITCHLOW,
MOSSCARR, HOLLINSCLOUGH, LONGNOR.

How are you Charles and all Mosscarr?
Since last we met the year's flown far,
'Twas at the Greenways wholesome bar
We passed an hour,
Till 'Time's' black cloud hid our fond star
And made us glower.

To your good wife I own I'm debtor,
Pray give regards from this my letter,
No warmer heart nor any better
Have I e'er known,
Her generous deeds a crown will get her
At her last home.

Young Richard oft of Robert speaks
And counts the days and then the weeks,
And eagerly the date he seeks
For Mosscarr's call,
The colour rushes to his cheeks
For your fond hall.

I've yet to have that eerie tale
About the cards the hooves and tail,
That lessons man whom Sabbaths fail
For evil's way.
Give me the facts - I'll rhyme and wail
The hours away.

The year flies on to Autumn's fall
And soon are kine chained to the stall
While out, the leaves all eddying fall
Upon the ground,
And naught is left from Summer's call
'Xept Robin's sound.

E'en now, ere Autumn's peeled the bough
And 'fore the sod has felt the plough
The waxing winds unruly bow
The oaken stem,
And clouds go racing past the brow
Of Cloudy Hen.

I trust the harvest fell your way -
I know it smiled on barns of hay -
And how your fields with hedgerows gay
Laughed with the sun,
Yet soon will summer fade away
And winter's come.

The twittering swallows will soon depart,
No more does Kingy flash and dart,
But fur and feather will fearful start
At crashing guns,
And bloody reek will quick the heart
Of Mars's sons.

The timorous hare safe with his speed,
The moorcock hid beneath the reed
Are overmatched when ball is freed
From murdering steel,
To satisfy some selfish need
That man may feel.

But pay no heed to my glum pen,
There's time enough 'twixt now and then
For friends to meet, o'er, o'er agen
Beside a fire,
In some snug tavern where the men
Have yarns for hire.

So till we meet and share the brew,
My fond regards to them and you,
And all the members of your crew
At lone Mosscarr,
A thought unites where hearts are true -
Though friends are far.

PERCY WILLIAMSON

A man he is with no mean frame
Of England's yeoman stock.
An artist-farmer of local fame
And steady as a rock.

His gnarled hands can take the plough,
Both pen and brush as well;
Creating beauty is his bent
As many men can tell.

The Well in Endon, at his touch
Like magic is transformed.
The grey-faced stone so hard and rough,
With greenery is adorned.

Fashioned is the old well's face
With floral motifs seen.
Portraits there depict life's race
And tributes to God and Queen.

Perhaps some poet's birth is told
Upon the facade there,
Or maybe victory's tales unfold
In Nature's colours rare.

No need is there for written scroll
The message to impart,
Enquiring eyes take in the whole
And marvel at the art.

Each portion tells its flowery tale
Remembrance to awake.
Uplifts the human heart so frail,
And inspires His word to take.

As years roll by and memories fade
The written word will stand,
His debt to life he will have paid
By his creative hand.

ENGLAND

The meadow flowers are blooming now
In England's fields and dells,
And scented zephyrs waft the brow
With rose and woodbine smells,
And insects tune their busy hum
Unending 'neath the tree,
And blackbird cries his wild 'larum
And flies away so free.

Each varied call that nature makes
Brings to the exile-guest,
A gentle tug that stirs and wakes
Dear England in his breast.
Emotions then the throat constricts,
The eye conglubes with tear,
The panting heart all else evicts
When thought of England's near.

'Tis summertime in England now
And plovers wheel and turn,
And songsters range upon the bough
And flying nestlings learn.
Dear island-home across the sea
My heart and mind embrace,
No other love like mine for thee
None shall thee e'er replace.

LAMENT FOR 'BIDDY', THE
AUTHOR'S PET GOAT

O! Biddy's ta'en the scours and died,
She's gone where ever good goats bide,
That's why I wander sad, red-eyed,
Because of my Biddy.

She came to me a winsome kid,
All frolicsome, I named her Bid'
"She'll grow a beard'.. they said - she did!
My handsome Biddy.

Her bleating voice hailed my footfall,
I answered best I could her call,
Now when I see her empty stall
I'm sad for Biddy.

Her firstling kid - a snow-white gem,
So proud she was of her first stem,
O! would that she were back ag'en,
My faithful Biddy.

She never failed to fill the pan,
Not like the other Black and Tan,
Who does her best, but never can
Out-rank my Biddy.

She wandered where the foxgloves blow,
Where haulms on green potatoes grow,
And Death's cold hand soon laid her low,
My peerless Biddy.

It was that wild and bell-like flower
That knelled for her earth's final hour,
Where e'er she's gone I pray that Power
Will tend my Biddy.

Yet tho' I grieve for her oftimes
And sing her praises in my rhymes,
I cannot hate those poison vines
That took my Biddy.

I found a spot where roses twine
With honeysuckle's scented vine,
Where courting brids o'er her may pine,
And there laid my Biddy.

Sweet myosotis tops her grave
And round the edge shy cowslips wave
And later, bees the roses crave,
All o'er my Biddy.

And when the wild flowers say goodbye,
I'll visit there with dewy eye
And let a cultured posy lie
On my poor Biddy.

My worldy life's experience shows
When God made Earth - each thing that grows,
The truest hearts He gave to those
Like honest Biddy.

So why should not her praise be sung?
Some men for less have topped life's rung,
And later, falsely propped, outflung
True-hearts like Biddy.

The lower orders know no guile,
(For Man's reserved the treach'rous smile)
I think that top the hircine file
They'll place my Biddy.

And when we all troop in to Court
To plead forgiveness, as we ought,
They'll nothing find who evil wrought
'Gainst those like Biddy.

LINES . . . .

If praise you have for a fellow man
Then sing it loud and long.
But if its only blame you have
Pray find a silent tongue.

LINES . . . .

Happy is the singing stream,
Bless'ed is the flower,
Playful is the bright sunbeam
After summer's shower.
How so happy can they be
When she my love's departed?
Dewdrops fall not from their e'e
Like from mine they're started.
Sings she not beside the stream
Where she once did wander,
Catching there the sultry beam
Where it rested, yonder.

THE ROYAL TOUR
FOR JUBILEE YEAR 1977

First to Scotia's bounding plain
Where white-capped summits touch the sky;
And crowded streets with cheering throngs
The silent mountains oft will vie.
The greetings from the loyal breasts -
The outstretched arm to friendly clasp,
The children with their garlands gay,
The hands that offer a warming grasp.

Then off to Cambria, Land of Song,
Who claim her Royal Son their own,
But first in Llandaff's cloisters kneel
For here each heart must be alone.
Each town and village line the way
With folk who come from far and near,
And some who only came to stare
Remain and later loudly cheer.

The sun resplendent for the tour,
Still keeps the azured skies so blue,
As Albion's fair and verdant land
Now waits to greet their Monarch true.
To dance and sing, with loyal toasts
Each subject calls her name so dear;
But when she looks toward Ulster's shores
They see her drop a silent tear.

THE GUEST

I suppose it was the cold and rain
That drove thee indoors my hearth to share,
To sample from my larder shelf
The bread and cheese that I keep there.

'Twould be alright to dine and go
But a week has past and thou'rt still here.
I warn thee mouse to get thee hence
Unworking bones are not fed here.

A hole exists in my waistcoat front
Where grease and ale has lodged each night.
I know by signs 'twas done by thee
Ungrateful wretch - nocturnal sprite.

Thou squeaking thief of poor man's bread
No mercy will I show for that,
My dearest garment - though soiled and worn -
Thou hast destroyed thou paltry sprat!

There's murder in my heart for thee
So take this warning while yet alive.
Both lime and trap - man's arts I'll try
To take thy life I will contrive.

And when I have thee in my power
I'll take thy hide of brown.
'Twill serve to patch the waistcoat hole
Thy gnawing teeth have ground.

AT DAWNING

When dawning tips the hills with red,
When larky sings with joy o'erhead,
When cottage doors smell sweet of bread
My heart is glad.
When cobbles ring the shire's tread
I'm never sad.

The rooks that cawing homeward fly,
The humming insects winging by,
The herdsman's call - the answering cry
I treasure dear.
The youthful scene tho' long passed by
Are ever near –

When winter wildly waves the trees,
When summer's blossom tempts the bees,
When schoolboy's kites ride high the breeze
What joy I feel.
When supper's ale and bread and cheese
I thankful kneel.

The gentle voices in the lane,
The joy of Love's first tender pain,
O' how I live them o'er again
With many a sigh
And offer rosebuds wet with rain
From a dewy eye.

O' DO YOU REMEMBER?

When dawn comes up and paints the sky
A gold and crimson red,
And when the larkling springs on high
Its heavenly songs to shed,
When o'er I smell the bloss'ming thorn
So gay with petals new,
An aching heart's within me born,
They mind me love of you.

A'down the clear and winding stream
How often would we stroll,
With hearts entwined in love's young dream
While willing lips console.
As words of love were softly spoke
I clasped you to my breast
And O! what passions we awoke
That seemed would never rest.

I wonder do you see the sky
And blossoms on the bough,
And do your dreams still form a tie
With youth, as mine do now,
And do some mem'ries wake within
Disturbing quiet rest,
And leaps your heart with madding din
At times when we loved best.

FRAGMENTS

After sinning and damation
Comes forgiving and salvation.

WILDBOARCLOUGH

The Dane is in her merry mood
She leaps the stony wier,
And sweeps the branches hanging low
With waters sweet and clear.

The rowanberries, red and ripe,
Along her banks adorn,
And mossy stones allow her ford
To fields of golden corn.

By yonder bridge, the sleepy cot
Lies nestling in the hill,
And pastured green encircling there
The rustic picture fill.

The murmuring sheep at twilight's close
The stream's unending flow,
Bring dusk and peace to all around
'Neath brooding Shuttlins Low.

ON THE 23rd PSALM

How sweet the vale of true content
Life's labours there to cease,
To tread the well-worn paths of truth
To know perpetual peace.

The restful scene of waters calm,
What joy to sit and gaze;
To see the restless world go by
In seeming mock amaze.

Enough - no more - just to sustain,
Possessions but a few;
To give, to share, to help and love,
To steer the cause that's true.

And then perhaps to rise no more,
Nor view the scenes around,
But finding still a lasting home
And laurelled be or crowned.

THISBE AND PYRAMUS

Thisbe the maid was beloved by Pyramus
Though parents forbade that she should,
They pledged there to meet by the tomb of Great Nimus,
Their hearts full of love and so good.

The maiden was first at the tomb on the hour
And saw there a lion so red,
Her garment she dropped at the carnivore's glower
And fawn-like to safety she fled.

Pyramus appeared at the place of the trysting
And saw where her garment did lie;
The spoor of the lion he saw through eyes misting
And in grief by his hand he did die.

Fair Thisbe returned to the spot from her cover
By the tomb of Great Nimus she crept;
At the sight of Pyramus she cried for her lover,
And cold by his side she soon slept.

THE NIGHTS DRAW IN

The night draws in with nipping cold
And hunger makes the brids grow bold,
And in the tavern tales are told
Around the fire,
While nightly frosts increase their hold,
And fields are drier.

The trees relenting bow the blast,
Long, long ago their leaves were cast,
And ricks are tied down hard and fast
'Fore Eastie draws,
The fields have given their all, and last -
Some measly straws.

The children hasten home from school
And round the hearth on chair and stool
They spoon their frumenty when cool,
And dream away,
About the gifts that are the rule
On Christmas Day.

The harvest-home has come and gone,
O how the moon that night it shone,
How many maids that had - have none
By giving all,
We'll see before next Wakes is yon,
When midwives call.

And those who think they may lose face
Across the hills and woodland race,
To fern-seed pick at rapid pace
And fill each jar,
So that, before they show disgrace,
They vanished are.

The stocks and tree stand in the square,
The village street is cold and bare
Except for lights that bleary glare
From castle wall,
The nuns their beads tell inside there -
So grim and tall.

The light's gone out where Annie sleeps,
The whirring owl its vigil keeps,
The moon across the churchyard creeps
With ghostly tread,
And near the wall some new-dug heaps
Await their dead.

THE POACHERS

On Diana's nights when the moon is bright,
And honest folk are abed,
They steal from each village and hamlet
With their nets and guns, and their bread.

Each one his nefarious trade will ply
While the old moon shines above.
Some conies take, some fishing go-
And others will feathers trove.

Dame nature's bounty is their own
They take it without praise;
And when that fruitful source o'erflows
No words of thanks they raise.

Comes dawn they homewards wend their way,
Each his own footways tread.
Lest someone see who should not know
How others earn their bread.

LETTER - TO L. HEATH. CHEDDLETON.

The Geometric Master came -
From vapour dust and burning flame
Dame Nature's whims he sought to tame,
He fashioned all.
Yet 'mongst those lowly of ill-fame
He made his stall.

He trod the rock-strewn arid road,
He spurned great fortune's cruel goad
Yet, for mankind He bore a load
Of high degree.
An ass's back - not Man's He rode
And made us free.

The lesson's there for all to choose,
To seek, to grasp, to win to lose.
To seize a star by any ruse
With selfish aim,
But, when we cast our mortal shoes
We heaven claim.

No doubt you fancied deviation
A'yond that of your present station;
But fie, O fie such elevation
Was ne'er your lot.
Life's level plain of transportation
Is all you got.

And yet just look from whence you came,
You've tasted labour, love and fame.
Unruly passion's had to tame
Like many another,
But then you've helped the sick and lame
Like christian brother.

So take another look at life,
Your home, each darling child and wife,
They're worth a world of wealth and strife
And tinsel glory,
Ambition holds a long, long knife
That's ever gory.

JEANIE

Jeanie's left me - gone for ever,
Never more with her to roam
Thro' the woodland, o'er the heather,
She has found her lasting home.

Who will teach the groves their singing?
In their sadness silent now.
Ne'er to hear their songs go winging
O'er the meadows from the bough.

Sweet she was like any flower,
Like the grass is after rain;
She has left her earthly bower
Filled with mem'ries causing pain.

Muted lapwings silent wheeling,
Merle and mavis quiet stand.
Muffled bells their message stealing
O'er the wintery summer land.

Broken-hearted here I wander,
Sweetest thoughts crowd in my mind,
Thoughts that with the years grow fonder,
Care and sadness left behind.

CHARLIE'S HUT

We all trooped home from school one day
When winter's hand gripped wild,
And trudged across the Brittle Waste
Where Nancy had her child.
Dead cats and dogs in the shallow pool
Once blown up round and bare
Were covered over by the snow
And now looked peaceful there.

We came up to owd Charlie's hut
Near covered by the drift,
'Twas made of railway sleepers, thick,
That earthquakes could not shift.
The tiny window at the side
Was clear of driving snow,
We planned to tap and have a game
Then quickly on to go.

We crept up to the glass, we four,
And looked from there, inside;
A candle burned, and what we saw
Caused gobs to gape out wide.
Poor Charlie lay across a chair
A carver on the floor,
While from his throat - a ghastly cut -
There dripped his own life's gore.
A yell went up from youthful throats,
We shivered with the fear,
Then turned and ran as each one thought
"Alone I'll not stay here".
We blabbed the tale to those at home
Who passed it on somewhere.
They took poor Charlie to the morgue
And held a P.M. there.

He died by his own hand, they said,
As if we didn't know.
But death was sure, apart from that,
For hunger laid him low.

A paper in his pocket told
That he must quit his shack,
This was, they said, the coup-de-grace,
The straw that broke his back.

The funeral was a dismal route,
But not unmourned went he,
For wreaths and flowers were on his bier
And there for all to see.
Some stood beside their own front door
As the horse-drawn hearse went by,
And red-eyed women dropped a tear
And rubbed a bleary eye.
And we cried too because they did,
We sensed the grief and shame,
For Charlie's medals numbered five
And he from war was lame.

His shack stood there for years and years,
'Twas used by man and beast.
And, O' if those rough walls could tell
My muse would have a feast.
But gossip now must take a hand
The picture to complete,
Your rustic bard had left the 'Hill,
'Fore th' next events we speak.
It seems that children played round there
When passing home from school;
And that 'twas haunted by a ghost
Appearing near to Yule.
It soon was known that lovers came
Where none could see or stare,
And many a child who passed that way
Was first conceived in there.

Soon drunkards used it out of spite,
And others 'taken short',
For Brittle Waste was wide exposed
And many folk were caught.
And so it came November fifth
They filled the shack with straw,
And on the top they placed a Guy -
O how the flames did roar,
Two days and nights the fire did last,
And when it fell to ash,
A rumour spread that those tough walls
Had held a mint of cash.

THE MERMAID

When the night casts its mantle o'er the moorland so grim
And the lone light is seen in the cot,
And the fire burns low in the old Mermaid Inn
As the evening's last tankard is got,
'Tis then that the Little Folk wait by the Pool
To see the fair Mermaid arise,
From down in the depths of her home black and cool
Can be heard her soft wailings and cries.

She rests with the Little Ones on the green hill
By the side of the lone misty road,
And they wait for the Horseman so spectral until
He has thundered past to his abode.
Then the Little Folk dance round the reedy-edged Pool
Till dawning will herald the day;
Then - POOF! they are gone each to its toadstool
And the Mermaid to waters so grey.

TO THEE

Cold the lips once red and burning,
Lips that seared when they touched mine.
Gone the smiles that set me yearning
For their taste more sweet than wine.

Where the green grass touched the streamlet,
Oft we sat on evenings fair,
Watched the willows wave their greeting
In the waters mirrored there.

Love was ours to hold and cherish,
Rarest jewel, brightest star,
Now neglected waits to perish
Like the wild rose carried far.

BLUE EYES - COLD HEART

Thy eyes are like the northern sea
As blue as Scotland's flower,
And when they turn their love on me
I wilt before their power.

Thy eyes are blue like northern sea's
Their amour I admit it,
Thy heart's just like the icy bergs
That sail so freely in it.

Can beams of light burn so with love
And hide a heart as cold,
Can flaming love and freezing charm
In one so sweet enfold?

ON THE PROSPECT OF CONFLICT
DURING THE DEPRESSION 1936

There is no work but there's the dole,
We freeze with cold for there's no coal.
Our belts are tighter each new day
And rents are owing where we stay.
Impoverished, of all pride bereft,
The Means Test took what bit was left,
We stand at corners scarecrowed yobs,
At home we eat but tea and pobs.
Our shoes gave out and now let in
And some of us have stooped to sin.
Aye', we've taken chonnucks from the field
And ate 'em raw when they were peeled.
We've poached the rabbits in Park Hall
And on their trout we've paid a call.
Their grain field rolls just like the sea -
A bit we've ta'en, for frumenty.
Don't wave the flag before our eyes,
Don't fill our ears with loyal cries,
Don't show us lords at glistening toasts,
Don't show us banquets wines and roasts.
And please don't call us as before
When you rich bastards start a war.
We've nought to fight, o'er nought to lose
Our needs in life you did refuse.
But we're not feared to lose our breath
The poor man's friend was ever Death.

THE ANGLER

He stands beside the water's edge
That reedy banks do hide,
And gazes at the waving fronds
That mark the currents glide.

And angled stem with goss'mer thread
Enjoins him to his prize -
A snick, a splash, an eddied pool
As out the union flies.

From day's first light he made his watch
And now reward is here,
He saw fond nature's daily tasks
In sequence true and clear.

The lark's first rise the blackbird's song
The moorhen searching there;
The one's who trip to slake their thirst,
All these to him are dear.

ENGLAND

O England of unrivalled spring
My thoughts are e'er of thee,
As now the blossom's hanging there
Upon the thorny tree.

The creamy bunch on rowans hang
Amid the sheltered glade,
Where bluebells, like an azured mist,
Full blooming stand displayed.

Bright buttercups and daisies fair,
The leas and meadows green;
They hide the nest that larky's made
Where deep some hoof has been.

Dear England, fairest of the fair,
Were thou to cast me down,
Before the strength had left my frame
On thee I'd place a crown.

TO THEE

Were I a linnet free and gay
I'd chant to thee my song each day.
Were I a lark each morn I'd spring
And from my tower thy praise I'd sing.

But even these would fail to show
How much for thee my love doth grow,
Not e'en the peacock's plumage bright
Can match thy beauty in my sight.

Not all the wealth that's known on earth
Can measure thee in trust or worth.
Thy heart's a gem of purest ray,
Thy voice is music's sweetest lay.

Ah Love! Sweet Love! my only pride
Is yet when thou art by my side.
My only joy from thee is given,
In thee I find my earthly heaven.

THE YELLOW BIRD

A yellow bird sat in a cage
And sang aloud with glee,
Surrounded by his gilded bars -
As happy as could be.
The sun was warm and the window, wide
Let out his tuneful lay,
O happy was the yellow bird
On that warm summer day.

A linnet came, and then a thrush
And perched by the window wide,
They closer hopped to the gilded cage
And shily peeped inside.
The yellow bird had shut his eyes
As he sang so loud and clear,
His throat swelled out with feathered pride
Like feline's fur with fear.

His song was done, he looked around
And saw his fellow mortals,
He hopped up to the topmost perch
And looked across the portals,
"I see you gaze with envy, friends,
At my exalted station,
And though we seem of different blends
I feel we are relation."

"O pray excuse our staring, friend,"
The throstle said, admonished,
"We heard your singing fine and loud
And really were astonished."
"I suppose for that you can't be blamed -
You look so drab and weathered,"
And as he spoke, the yellow bird
Displayed, so finely feathered.

"I'm housed and fed in this fine cage,
I want for nothing ever,
The tender thread of life for you
One winter's blast could sever,"
The linnet's eye blinked once or twice,
He curtsied 'fore his betters,
"These gilded bars round your domain -
They also are your fetters."

His wing he swept out like an arm,
And pointed to the vista,
"But we've all this, and more beside,
That Freedom gives us, Mister.
'Tis true that cold and hunger bite,
And time for us flies faster,
But yet I fear those bars the more -
More yet, I fear your master."

THE SONS OF ENGLAND

In many lands across the sea
The sons of England lie,
The sons of England brave and true,
Whom Duty called to die.

In steaming swamps and jungles dark,
In deserts open wide,
Those foreign soils without a mark
Their precious bones may hide.

Their mem'ries tho' our hearts imbue
Tho' far away they lie;
Those sons of England stout and true,
Whom duty called to die.

WINTER

The icy snow hangs in the trees
And howling blasts go wildly by,
The hives hold snug their clustered bees
The rooks alone haste o'er the sky.

Amid the hedge the robin sits
His hungry brethren perched besides,
The restless owl tu-whoo tu-whits
And from his eyrie swiftly glides.

The ermined fields all starkly bare
Hold secrets till the light of day,
Then in the snow they mark Jack Hare
And point his restless wandering way -

He moved to where the ricks are moored
Where breached the mangold mounds are seen,
Such tiny morsels ne'er are scored
Nor missed before, nor since have been.

Great Architect of heaven and earth
Who made all things above, below,
Whose will controls all death and birth
Who points the way that all things go -

If ever I should grudge my lot
Or scorn a fellow-mortal's woe,
Or envy those who wealth have got
While I have nothing for to show -

Then point to me the beast and bird
Whom Thou hast placed below Thy man,
Who evidence Thy humble word
And make the best of what they can -

I'll silence every rebel thought
That enters my untutored mind,
I'll keep the lesson nature's taught
And through her teaching Thy ways find.

But, Lord, if I'm to be a slave
To move when someone may behest,
Why didst Thou place a spirit bold
And independent in my breast?

O SWEET DOVE

Blow gently warm zephyrs across her bright water
And stem you impatience you swift-bending wave,
How can my mere words win the heart of my dearie
When your tender music's the sound that we crave.

No maid can resist all the beauties you offer,
No eyes without passion can view your great charm,
A heart that is placid will bound with confusion
A spirit so cautious will sound an alarm.

The gay sportive dry in your pools rush and frolic
While zealously anglers bend o'er your stream;
The sunbeams a measure dance to your soft murmur
While you, O my muse, evoke me to dream.

The sweet smelling briars your green banks adorning
The tall trembling aspens entwine up above;
The loveliest of nature salutes you each dawning
And I pen my homage to you, O sweet Dove.

To Douglas Holdcroft, Recorder.

These..............

ON THE ANNUAL GATHERING OF
THE OLD NORTONIAN SOCIETY.

The evening found an early start
And all were wined and dined;
The fond re-unions touched the heart
And absent friends were pined.
The President paid fond regards
When Cadman was installed,
And from the lips of Corfield - bard,
Sweet Devon was extolled.

Our staid Recorder then made note
Of a life fast disappearing,
The fields of green had shed their coat,
Estates and roads appearing.
An urban tone was creeping fast
Replacing rural scenes
That sadly bow before the blast
To rise ne'er more it seems.
To compensate us for this loss
He spoke of fresh new faces
(An ill-got change, this human dross,
For Nature's charms and graces.)

We then heard Bourne and Critchlow speak,
Ralph Jack - Carruthers too;
They praised the Councils, Stoke and Leek,
('Twas seemly so to do.)
Endon found voice in her fine sons
Who at the feast was guests,
The artist-farmer Williamson,
And Perkins spoke with zest.

The platform warmed to barley-mow
When Glass got to his feet;
The welkin rang for the Medico,
His oratory - a treat.
His tales so mirthful pleased the mind,
Will never be forgot.
He superscribed for life's dull bind
"Of laughter, take a lot".

But Time's unwelcome hand did turn
Though Care had bit Adieu!
The hours sped by ne'er to return
So happy was our crew.
And as we said a fond farewell
And joined in 'Auld Lang Syne',
Across the hall a hush it fell –
Bob Midwinter cried, "TIME"!

TO THE BRIAR ROSE

I grasp with joy thy trembling spray,
And gently pull it down,
To catch the scent from petals gay,
That on thy stems abound.

The wild bee ranges o'er thy flowers
His nectarous quest fulfilled,
The linnets choose thy thorny bowers
When tiny homes they build.

Sweet briar-rose so wild and free,
The pride of summer time,
Such tender thoughts have I for thee
When e'er I see thy vine.

TOM'S GRANNY

Summer days were long and fine
And meadows sweet with hay,
And richer folk had gone to sea
To spend their holiday.
But never would we change them that
For days down on the farm -
The chance to ride Owd Bob to grass,
Was our behaviour's charm.

Five days we worked, the hay was in,
Our limbs were brown and strong.
We fetched the cattle home at night
With many a happy song.
Then to our homes we'd wend our way,
Two pennies jingling loud
Young Tom and I were such good pals -
Quite different from the crowd.
Our journey home was spent in talk
Of toast and dripping bread.
A penny to our Mams we'd give,
The rest on sweet Scotchbread.

And so for two whole weeks and more,
We toiled till night had come,
We'd over eighteen-pence apiece,
A most tremendous sum.
'Twas Saturday, I mind it well,
We homeward made our way,
Through Miggie's fields and Old Top Nog,
Near closing time of day.
Just down the street by Pinky's shop
We turned to say goodnight,
When by Tom's door we saw a crowd
Our hearts beat mad with fright,
The doctor and police were there,
We quickly joined the crowd

When Addie Simpson turned us back
Her face was sad and cowed.
"You come with me", she said to Tom,
And turned him round about,
Into her house she took the boy,
I then heard someone shout.

I turned and saw a group of men
March out from Granny's door,
And in between them, there she lay,
So bony, sad and poor.
Her face was plain through her black shawl,
It had a bluish tinge,
Her long black apron, worn and thin,
Hung round her bony limbs.
Tom's father stood on their front step
All miserable and sad.
The two young sisters, five year twins,
Clung round the legs of dad.

The noble family stood in grief,
The parent with each child.
What thoughts were racing through his mind,
What schemes, or fancies wild?
Perhaps he thought of France's mud,
The blood and sweat and tears,
And of his body, broken there,
And of the following years.
When lungs destroyed by gas turned sour,
Consumption set from then,
Unwanted by the pit for work
Whose choice was fitter men.
Then he'll remember, at this time,
Of Martha's loving care,
Of how she scrubbed and worked outside
To earn some honest fare.

Of little things the houses gave
To show her work was good,
And how the Means Test later came
To suck and sell their blood.
Miss Cook, the teacher's wireless went,
They insisted on its sale,
A bicycle on which she rode,
They all must go - or jail.
One could not claim allowances
With luxuries to hand,
The days of heroes now had passed,
O Traitor thou, England!.
How Martha's work increased with time,
She little had herself,
And when the children came along
No need for pantry shelf.
The twins were born one winter, cold,
No coal was there for fire.
Too proud to beg, too weak to fight,
She sank into Death's mire.

Her mother left her attic bare
To come and stay and fend,
But soon she gave up, broke with age,
And last goodbyes she penned.
She turned the oven gas on full,
But fate's a wicked jade,
The gas ran out before her breath
And she escaped the shade.
This last, though, Granny had made sure,
Four pennies she had tried,
For death is the most certain cure
Of ills the poor must ride.

THE WATERCRESS MAN

With a large wicker basket full brimming with green
That hangs round his waist where the leather is seen,
Each bright Sunday morning when the season is there
He strolls round the village a'crying his ware.

His trousers are patched and with knee-strings are tied,
And his jacket is shiny with pockets so wide.
He wears big leather boots over stockingless feet
That clatter and spark as he walks down the street.

The old and infirm who to bedroom are fast
Press their face to the pane just to see him go past,
And list to his voice - like a sweet serenade -
His presence is one of which memories are made.

The children run to him with platter or pan
And a penny they give to the watercress-man
Who fills what they bring with fresh cresses so green
While he sings out its praise for the back and the spleen.

By noon tis all gone and he wends on his way,
The watercress-man with his basket of grey,
But he will return when the season is there
Down the old cobbled street he will sing out his ware.

Some bright Sunday morn hear his iron-shod feet
And the sound of his voice as he walks down the street,
Then the village will wake to the song of his ware
And the watercress-man once more will be there.

ABERFAN

(the author was present at this disaster)

The morning mists clung to the face
Of Merthyr's winding vale,
The noisy Taff went hurrying by
While skies were stilly pale.
Black Friday 'twas, October time,
The autumn time of year,
When harvests from the earth are in
Ere winter's blasts so drear.
The mountains wreathed in deathly shrouds,
Man's architecture there,
Like giant molehills, wretched, black,
All treeless, grassly bare.
And lower down from house and farm
They made their morning way
Along the paths and pavements cold,
'Twas schooling-time of day.

Each classroom rang with early prayer
As gently voices raised
A solemn tribute to His love,
Their anthems swelled with praise.
Did'st hear those tiny voices? Lord,
They lifted them for Thee,
They sang of Thine Begotten Son
Who took them to His knee.
And while the silence o'er them lay -
Each to a desk they stood -
The mountain moved towards their doom
Engulfed them in its flood.

The prayers were said, the cries too late,
The lambs to slaughter came,
O God! to whom we owe our life,
For this who shall we blame?
O! who will point the finger first?
Who'll cast the angry stone?
Who shall in guilt be first arraigned?
Who will accuse - atone?
But who can move a mountain, Lord?
But Thou, and here I stay,
For heavy hearts and bitter tears
Mark that unholy day.

They reach Thy heaven from all the earth,
No colour, creed, or vow,
The innocent with guilty stand
And 'fore Thy throne they bow.
Some die in battle, some in toil;
All reach Thee tho', that can,
We pray Thee in Thy goodness keep
Each soul from Aberfan.
And let their epitaph run thus:
(If epitaph there be)
Raze to the earth those blackened piles
From fear set them free.
Their memory-stone must not be raised
'Midst heaps of slag and slime,
They loved the valley's greener fields
Its spring and summertime.
And you who think on Aberfan,
All you who there abide,
For pity's sake the future heed,
Or 'twas in vain they died.

HERO AND LEANDER

At Abydos dwelt a youth Leander,
Who to Sestor did once meander,
The Temple of Venus nearby lay
And he entered in to kneel and pray.
While at devotions he did see
A young priestess of rare beauty,
And he poured forth to her his love
Which both they pledged by stars above.
Their trysting-times they secret made
For if their plot had ere been laid
Fair Hero and her love would die;
But every night to meet they'd try.

Upon the tower so high above
Sweet Hero hung her lamp of love
To guide Leander across the sea,
Each night he swam most expertly.
The darkly hours they sped away,
Their love ne'er knew the time nor day.
One night fair Hero set her light
Upon the tower it burned full bright,
And she impatient sat below
And glowed as only lovers glow.
Outside she heard no sigh or sound,
Nor did she know false wind had found
Their secret, and with jealous rage
Had killed the light within the cage.
And Hero sat with heart aglow
While there outside the wind did blow.

Leander, full of love and free,
Across the Hellespont swam he,
And when he still had much to cross
The darkness told him of his loss.
He swam thereon without a sign
For Hero then his heart did pine.
His strength ebbed fast till 'twas no more,
And later there upon the shore
His youthful form - safe from the blast,
By Wind and wave thereon was cast.
The stricken priestess moaned her loss
Till from the cliff herself did toss,
And there within the angry sea
Leander found his Hero - free.

TO.......................

Moon of my gladness
Radiant and bright,
Driving all sadness
Far from my sight.

Splendorous adornment,
An aura of bliss,
Queen of my firmanent,
I long for your kiss.

Your touch, I'm enraptured,
Your voice is a song,
My heart have you captured,
To you I belong.

ON SEEING A NEST OF LARKS
DESTROYED BY A MOWING MACHINE

What can I do to ease the pain
That stabs my heart again again;
No words of mine can hide the shame
I'm feeling now,
O'er all the earth it's man to blame
For every row.

The morning bright saw thee above
And chanting out thy song of love,
And later fluttering gently hove
Upon thy tower,
Yet grounding far beyond thy dove
In feath'ry bower.

Thy notes awake the sleepy croft
And night attire is quickly doffed,
With woodbine's scent they inward waft
To cosy room,
And morning-window's flung so oft
To chase the gloom.

Yet now the one whom thou dost cheer
Has ravaged what you both hold dear
Your nest - and nestlings gone I fear
Before the knife,
She bravely stayed till it came near
To end her life.

Then with a screech of heartfelt pain
I saw her lift and leave the plain,
No doubt that spot will ne'er again
Hear thy glad voice,
And I who saw it all I fain
Will ne'er rejoice.

Beyond the woodland see the hill,
There meadows lie unmown and still;
They've never cut it yet - nor will,
It's feg and marsh,
Pray hasten there some hollow fill,
Here life's too harsh.

Find some bit hollow round and snug
Which long ago some hoof has dug,
Where warm she'll lie like any spug
Safe in the gorse,
Where lain-up kine sparse grasses tug
And ageing horse.

And warn the others of thy train
Who yet may choose the unmown plain,
That man must never wait on rain
When barns are void,
His all depends on creaking wain
And stacks deployed.

The elements may rob him yet
If grass or grain is gathered wet
So he may join thee soon to fret
At losses dear,
While at his door some gnawing debt
Is ever near.

Now Larky there I've tried to show
That man still bears the greater woe,
And as your heartstrings heal, I know
You'll be forgiving,
For pain and anguish - e'en death's blow
Is part of living.

THOSE GRACIOUS HALLS

Fair Oxford's spires delight the eye
Her halls of learning too,
And Cambridge with all else will vie
Her scholars get their due.
And many more in this fair isle
Teach wisdom just the same,
But they be schools in lesser file,
Unsung, unheard their name.

In some back street of dingy rows
The lowly buildings stand,
Inside the desks are piled in rows
Without the frills so grand.
The chalk and blackboard stick and hat,
The tools of master's trade,
The long high seat where dunces sat
And heard his loud tirade.

The pupils trip each weekly morn
Still tired from early toil
And chant the prayers to Saviour born
(Some cannot sleep long foil)
The lessons drag on hour by hour
And Shakespeare's learn'd by heart,
Till mem'ry speaks of Gaunt's last hours
Or tells Macbeth's black art.

Algebraic phrases take their turn
The stick will rise and fall
And frozen hands to life will burn
For Gibbon's Decline and Fall.
Pythagoras is later given
Inside another room,
And some are well nigh nearly riven
Where Science has its tomb.

The test,

Both oxygen and aqua part by adding acid nitric
Then passing through an electric spark
But mind it's not ignited.
A fearful bang ensues at that the laden jars are shattered,
And all the contents of the vat
On grubby faces spattered.

But classrooms are the sterner part
Of a lowly education,
Athletics cheer the dreary heart
Cause joyful exclamation.
Around the field they chase the wind
They lunge and kick and scamper
Until the whistle ends their stint
(Now discipline will hamper)

In file aglow they march untired,
Discussing, argumentive,
Pursue the points the game has fired
Alert now and attentive.
And sometimes anger takes the field
And strength there wins the day,
But all this quickly there is healed
As time wings on its way.

And so they go from day to day,
'Til fourteen summers passing
They leave the school so dull and grey,
To join a force that's massing.
To seek for work in fact'ry, mine,
Or till the happy land
(Tho' there rewards not silver shine
But toil - and beauty's hand.)

Some drift along life's dreary way
Forgetting earlier studies,
And school and youth seem far away
They're now so many bodies
To serve their land in time of war
And after that their master,
The one may take their good red gore
The other brings age faster.

But some pursue the learning quest
When toil has ended day,
And turn aside from fool's behest
To fritter hours away
By following pleasures tainted, dim,
That quickly turn so sour
And make life's outlook black and grim
And cull the lovely flower.

These then the lowly schools produce
And life will shape their way,
And naught that comes will e'er reduce
What minds store every day.
Their common sense is quickly seen
Where the learned and they foregather,
For they across both paths have been,
The poor and rich together.

O WHY

Why do the coverts silent stand?
'Tis Spring, they should be ringing;
Ah yes, they hear the sweeter song
Of Dora Capey, singing.

THE HEADLESS HORSEMAN

The misty miles of heathered heath stretch over hills and vales
From Three Shires Head and Swythamley to Dove's green grassy dales.
The sodden turfs by Mermaid's Pool - beside the lonely road -
May nourish hard bell-wethers and shelter witches toad.
The noisy winds blow eeriely free across the cloudy moors
Where ' tis said a horseman rides disdaining nature's laws.
'Pon spectral horse with speed of wind dressed for another age
The ghostly rider gallops on ere moon hath set her stage.

Many a luckless stranger has crossed the weary moor
And seen the sight that makes men fear and hounds like lions roar.
(For all who look on things so strange the evil takes their brain)
Demented man and sightless hound roam piteous o'er the plain;
Until some kindly husbandman will lead them to his cot,
There to rest and bide twelve moons till mind's sanity is got.
Then he will tell the same sad tale of riding o'er the moor
And seeing the Headless Horseman - as many have done before.

The legend has it that he'll ride for ever and the day.
Some say 'twas murder set him forth upon his headless way;
While others dreamily whisper that he was crossed in love,
And died at the hand of a rival as he rested by the Dove.
His head was severed from his neck to spoil a knowing gaze;
And his steed ran through with bladed steel and left to time's wastage.
And since the time of Charles the First he's galloped o'er the moor,
Past Mermaid's Pool - on moonlight nights - he rides for ever more.

HEZEKIAH

A Tale

On the hillside by the Dallas,
There lived Hez so cold and callous.
By the dark forboding forest
Where the green grass gew the lushest.
As a hermit in his cottage,
All alone except for Drerda -
Drerda of the mighty bellow,
Glaring eyes, one blue, one yellow.
Ne'er before was such as Drerda,
Long ago there was the murder,
In the wood the body lifeless
Left old Hez bereft and wifeless.

The tale:

About the cot one morning winging
Went Maggie to her duties singing.
Hez and Drerda silent stealing
Where the teal-duck came in wheeling.
Came a knock that fateful morning,
There stood dark-skinned man all fawning
Pleading begging for a penny
But Maggie said she had not many.
Asked him in and food she gave him
And the coat her father laid in
When his corpse from lake was brought in
He the wild duck had been hunting.
After she had fed and clothed him
Food to take she gladly spared him,
Then with female intuition
Searched his face and saw a vision.
On the forehead of the strange man
Sprouted horns like those of Satan.

Red his eyes shone like the ember
That lastly dies inside the fender.
Maggie backed at sight so fearsome
Prayed for help - full well did need some,
Clutched her beads as if she knowing
That her sands were fastly flowing.
Not a scream or groan she uttered
As his knife her flesh deep rutted;
Sank she to the pinewood flooring
On her breast a ghastly goring.
Searched he then the little bower
(At the corpse he oft did glower)
Finding then the pot of money
On the table threw a penny.
Lifted he the corpse of Maggie
O'er his shoulder limp and baggy.
Strode into the darkening forest
From the spot where grass grew lushest.
On and on without a murmer
Where the trees closed in more firmer,
Then when far from sight and hearing
Stopped and rested in a clearing.
Made a fire took meal with leisure
That giver gave with utmost pleasure.
Meanwhile old Hez with Drerda guiding
Pathway thro' the bog was finding.
Of the game found goodly traces
Laden he with four good braces.
When at last they found firm grounding
Away went Drerda loudly sounding,
Joyful to the cot was making
All the glen his echoes breaking.
Then silence fell and Hezekiah
With a look of fear so dire
To the doorway greatly hastened
Saw the room, the floor and casement
Knelt and touched the blood so soggy,
'Fore his eyes the mist rolled foggy,
Saw the knife with blood so gouted

Turning then to Drerda shouted.
Bounding in came giant canine,
Whimpered, smelled then made a pathline,
Crossed where grasses grew the lushest
To the woody darkened forest;
Hez then bade the dog be silent,
Followed on - knew what each sign meant.
Where the body touched the greenleaf
Followed they the murdering sneak-thief
Till at last old Hez saw Drerda
Stand by him that did the murder.
But from him came no restraining
As Maggie there his heart was paining.
Drerda stalked with mane erecting
Twitching tail and muscles flexing
Teeth so big and white was baring
Eyes of blue and yellow glaring.
The man, if such he were, was stalking
Round and round the clearing walking,
Fingers long and stiff and curling
Such a sight it was un-nerving.
Hez looked on with sight un-seeing,
Like a man whom life is fleeing,
Like those who practise necromancy
Speak to the spirit whom they fancy.
Drerda snarled and roared to battle,
Grasped man-devil by the hackle,
Ripped the flesh down to the knuckle
But all he gave was devilish chuckle.
Another bound Drerda leapt catching
Bore him down while biting, scratching,
Grasped his neck in jaws so tightly,
Shook him like he weighed so lightly.
Shook as the rat is by a terrier,
Shook and tightened more and merrier.
Till with a crack and combat ended,
And neck was broke where ne'er tis mended.
Hez awoke with fright from dreaming
Like a babe he lay down screaming,

All his sorrow then poured from him
All his wishing and his wondering.
Then he saw the horned man-devil
Downward turned face in the gravel.
Turned him with a foot so wary
Lest he see some thing so scary.
He then saw something - ne'er forgetting
Come to that face once horns begetting.
From bestial visage none so meaner
It changed to beauty none serener.
With fear Hez let his mouth grow wider
Without a thought what may betide her,
Left both corpses in the clearing
Ran with Drerda his saneness fearing.
Ran they through foreboding forest
To where the green grass grew the lushest.
Hez then stopped in dumb amazement
As wood smoke rose from chimney 'scapement.
Slowly crossed to there with Drerda-
Where the gore would tell of murder.
Heard a woman gaily singing,
Ag'ed throat the notes sent winging.
Hasty stepped he to the doorway,
Saw no knife upon the floorway,
Only a stool and Maggie spinning
Turned to him with smile so winning.
Then he told her all his story,
The corpse, the man and knife so gory.
But she only burst out laughing
Fondly nudged him gaily chaffing.
Day by day he told his story
Of the corpse and knife so gory,
More and more she lightly chaffed him,
More and more his temper grew thin.
Till one day while repast taking
Maggie still her fun was making,
Wild and wilder arms were flinging
Through the air the knife was singing.
Maggie never felt the stabbing,

Through her heart the knife went jabbing;
Sank she to the pinewood flooring
Fast and faster gore was running.
Hez looked down with eyes now bolder
Threw poor Maggie o'er his shoulder,
Set he forth to darkened forest
Crossed the green where grass grew lushest.
Stalked behind him faithful Drerda
Silent witness to the murder.
Followed he old Hezekiah
Doomed his soul to lasting fire.
Left her body in the clearing,
Left no trace of guilt revealing,
Then he back to lonely bower,
His fear was mounting hour by hour.
Till he told his sadly story
But all trace of signs so gory
Vanished from his tiny bower
Liked petals fall from cutted briar.
The searchers through the woodland peering
Found no trace amid the clearing.
Then they thought that Hezekiah
Sought to make them fret and ire.
Nor was traced his line or birthright
Though the keeper wearched a whole night.
Nor was trace found in the bower
Of a loom or female power.
Nor had any person seen her
Where the grasses grew the greener,
By the dark forbidding forest
Where the grasses grew the lushest.
So they left him there to ponder
If he ere took body yonder
To the forest and the clearing,
Or was mind a fancy rearing.
But the story as he told it
Spread around the tiny hamlet,
How old Hez and faithful Drerda
Were concerned in queerest murder.

Murder where no one was murdered.
And twice-dead Maggie mystery furthered.
So twas thought she just existed
In the mind of Hez so twisted.
Down the years the tale was handed
With fear the lake and Dallas branded.
Prospered by the lips of mother
Who told each child - who tell each other
At firesides when nights are longest,
When the north wind blows the strongest.
The child at night finds no reposing
As infant mind distorts; and growing,
Till fear as bad as any colic
So lightly in the head will frolic.
And ghosts of Maggie, Hez and Drerda
Perform again the ghastly murder.

EMMA'S SPELL

Old Emma lives in the tumbled cot
Her years unknown though 'tis a lot;
The grand old men now hoary grey
Remember her when boys were they
And she was then as they are now,
The many years have marked her brow.

They used to fetch her long ago
When birthing pangs began to show,
And many a man recalls those nights
So late and cold, with lantern lights
To Emma's cot to hammer hard
And hear the door with noise unbarred.

The old ones say she is a witch
And meets her brethren by Deep Ditch;
And that 'twas through her evil spell
Poor Hatty in the water fell.
For it was known they'd lovers been
Till she caught him with Garter Jean.

One night while we were taking ale
Wap Curtis told us such a tale.
How he and Jane were walking late
And lingered long by five-barred gate,
Until the moon was riding low
And stars were then a fitful glow.
He saw them riding from the moon,
Five witches all astride one broom.
They went behind old Emma's cot
And Wap so near could see the lot.
Before he went on with his tale
Wap shuddered, then took draught of ale.

Inside where bright the hearth did burn
There boiled and spat the lobby urn.
He saw them place in boiling pot
Some things which from their cloaks they got,
An hare, some frogs and newts as well
And then they seemed to cast a spell
And mumbled words which were not clear,
Then, Wap said, he quaked with fear.
For loud they spake not once but twain,
And he heard the sound of Hatty's name.
Not many weeks had come and gone
'Fore Hatty went with boots still on.

The Wap continued with his tale
How he one night got full of ale,
And doleful thought of Hatty's end
And how for years he'd been a friend.
He staggered down to Emma's door
And called her witch and devilled-whore;
She threatened him if he should cant
He would be changed from man to ant.

At this he sobered like a judge
And back from whence he came did trudge;
Nor mentioned he to living soul
For of the ant he'd taken toll;
And he liked not the endless work
(For Wap was one who tried to shirk)
But the vicar charmed the tale from him
And calmed his fear and trembling limb
And said that only Him above
Could cast a spell and 'twould be love.

Then all our thoughts unsaid did linger,
While with slopped ale and bony finger
Old Tipper drew five witches features
And made them look such eerie creatures.
All across the old deal table
Scrawled those beldams drawn so able.
Complete with hats and noses pointed
And each one to the other jointed.
Old Wap looked down before they dried
And twice to raise himself he tried
But he fell back with rolling eyes
Like someone shook with great surprise.
With brandies large he came around
And took his place but made no sould.
And thus we passed the night away
All solomn looked who once were gay.

Now when he works down on the farm
No ant need fear a single harm,
For Wap still thinks of Emma's spell
And nothing will his fears quell.
He sees the toiling insect horde
Rushing thither across the sward
And wonders if a choice gave she
He may prefer to be a bee.
For what they ate was much preferred
To chewed up muck the ants interred
And left until with fungi grown,
The thought alone would turn a stone.
And so through life he carries on
No ant need far 'till Emma's gone,
He ploughs around the ant-hill dome
For there he fears is his next home.

ON FINDING A ROBIN FROZEN
TO DEATH IN A TREE

The Wintry wind blew full each day
And turned rock hard the mushy clay,
Folk hastened home while yet they may
To flee the storm,
Lest cold and darkness might delay
Them there forlorn.

The east had howled both day and night
His icy teeth with pain did bite,
The lain-out kine hugged up in fright
And lowed with fear,
The bleary morn a welcome sight,
And none more dear.

The snow and ice filled hedge and nook,
The earth wore winter's deathly look,
I passed the bridge at Stockton Brook
All clammy cold,
A bottle now, as lief't as look
'S worth more than gold.

I mused aloud upon my state
Then thought of those of worser fate,
Poor brids I thought, who had to wait
On gen'rous man,
The meagre droppings from his plate
Take when they can.

My mind was thinking on it still
And sentimental thoughts did fill,
When in a thorn a'top Moss Hill
So cold and drear
A huddled form I spied, with will
I stepped up near.

The tiny feet in frozen state
Still clutched the perch whereon it sate,
I freed the left - and then its mate,
'Twas stiff to hold,
I fear my efforts were too late -
By hours old.

I guessed the night had seen it die
With no-one near to hear its cry,
No tears will fall from loving eye
For thee, poor Robin,
Dame Nature's ways seem all awry
And cause much sobbin'.

What harm did'st thou upon the earth
To make grim eastie rob thy birth?
Thy rosy breast - did'st know its birth
Was Royal Blood?
And none can peer thy song or worth,
Nor ever could.

Yet here to fit some scheme or plan
Thou'rt made to suffer just like man.
We try evade but never can,
Life's fortunes ill,
We see the writing - ne'er the han'
That holds the quill.

Oftimes when moithered by the run
I've wondered why it all begun,
And if ill-fortune jumped the gun
My starter fired,
For round my life a web he's spun
Since I was sired.

But when my pockets jingle loud
I mingle happy with the crowd,
I cock my finger at the shroud
That's waiting near.
To care I'll never bend I've vowed,
However near.

And then again I've seen the day
When things ne'er take their rightful way,
I've wondered if the morning may
Find me aloft,
And then a change will come to stay
Within my croft.

So Robin rest content with that,
Old eastie's saved thee from the cat,
Tho' which is worst - each one's a twat
And equal fate,
Life's span's no longer than a gnat
Come soon or late.

O! happy those whose life ahead
Can never cause them fear nor dread,
Who pay no heed to what is said
By Book or law,
And yet have meat and bins of bread,
And more in store.

SNOWDROPS

Snowy white they come ere springtime,
Winter's hand still holds the rein,
While the trees stand bare and silent
Marking clear the winding lane.

Spring they promise round the corner,
Winter's gloom will soon away,
Trudging from the greening landscape
Farther, faster with each day.

O what joy your presence bringing,
Hope for future plans behold,
Nature's magic quick transforming
Dark despair to precious gold.

THE GIPSIES BURNING

Where the rocky headland ends the wood
And the gloomy cave for centuries stood,
And unfathomed pit its secrets hold
(In there at night dead bodies rolled).
'Twas such a night when owlets fly
And fill the air with eerie cry;
And bats take wing and leave the cave
And ghosts rise up from pitty grave.

A gypsy camped by the woodland edge,
His family - five - all safe abed,
When a figure moved by the rocky wall
Then o'er the green began to crawl.
The man - for such it was - then stood
Where late a rooster shed its blood;
By the steps that lead to the painted door
He softly stepped from the grassy floor.

Then he looked around with a furtive gaze
And the moon shone full on a grave visage,
He fingered a knife with a shining blade
And opened the door, not a sound he made,
He later left with a large limp sack
That he threw across his scrawny back
And made his way to the gloomy pit;
Six times betwixt the two did flit.

The piebald horse that grazed nearby
He harnessed up with a hasty sigh,
Onto the lane so wary drawn,
Then away he drove to meet the dawn.
That fate to him dealt a cruel blow
The evil man was not to know.
The road he took with the caravan
Would lead him to the tribal clan.

Just as the sun with gold brought day
He saw and knew of his error'd way,
Too late he saw the dark-skinned men
With hostile gaze regarding him.
They stayed the horse with tightened rein
And searched the van and found the stain,
Then grasped the man with ne'er a word
Though fierce looks showed hearts were stirred.

They placed the van on an open green
And the man was laid where their kin had been,
Then they stacked the brushwood around and o'er
Till the caravan was seen no more.
And in the holocaust that followed
Died man who in man's blood had wallowed.
The curious folk who with questions ran
Were told 'twas a beacon in honour of Pan.

To make the sign that all was good
They danced as only the gipsies could,
And fiddles were played as if ne'er to tire
As the evil man went from fire to fire.
Ere after that - so the tale is told -
When Pan with pipes will tune the grove,
The fiddlers will that greensward tread
And the gipsies dance as the sky glows red.

But no-one dares to tread the grove
Where evil man by fire shrove,
Nor take the road near unfathomed pit
Where owlets fly and flitmice flit.
When they hear the pipes on the still night air
And the fiddles play, they know that there
Near the open green will be the fire
With ghostly dancers that never tire.

OWD BOB

I knew him when a lad - but nine,
And massive was he then,
His towering frame left little room
Betwixt each shaftling stem.
Deep chestnut was his shining coat
And black his mane and tail,
His star was white as driven snow,
His fetlocks, starry pale,
No shire could match him in the field
The plough seemed but a toy
As fast the furrows fell behind
The brown-skinned horse and boy.
The hay-wain too pitched three forks high
He moved with ease and grace,
"Come on, Owd Bob," the children called,
As to and fro they raced.

They fed and watered him each round
And tiny palms would feel
The soft warm nose pressed gently there
For pear or apple peel.
His feats of strength were far renowned
And crowds once bet in vain
When to a tractor Bob was led
With traces-gear and chain.

The flag was dropped, the engine roared,
The chain went taut and sang,
"Come on Owd Bob", the rustics cried
As leathers snapped their twang.
No goad was needed for that back
His legs of oak spread wide,
His hooves of steel bit deep the loam
The engine roared and cried.

Full throttle now with noisy din
But not one inch he moved.
The boy stood placid at his head
While tractor wheels deep grooved.
And then it came - the lad stood back,
And "Up, Owd Bob," he cried.
The crowd all stood in silence then
With mouths agaping wide.

Owd Bob with nostrils wide and flared
Sank belly down to earth
Then seemed to arch and round his back
Then forward, sudden lurch.
And he went on - the tractor came,
The match was o'er and won,
And city slickers paid their due
Unto each rustic son.
And many days they talked of Bob
And of that village green,
Where nature's beauty, strength and grace
O'ercame the iron machine.

He's pastured now and honest toil
Has brought its rich reward,
In sweet content with age'd ease
He grazes on the sward.
The rich brown coat has left his back
His star has faded too,
His stand betokens years of toil
His lip has dropped askew.
But still the proud light's in his eye
His neck's arched as of yore,
How quick the years have flown away,
Come five, he'll be two-score.

Beset by Nature's noblest arts
With strength and beauty graced,
Where is the soul-less knave of hearts
Who'd have these joys replaced?

THE OLD SOW

They sat in the tavern with their tankards before them
And the thick blackened smoke billowed out up above them,
The dominoes clicked on the ale-stained old table
And some played the crib while mind was yet able.
When into the tavern stepped two ladies, genteel,
Ordered water, then one turned around on her heel
Took the road to the passage so dark and so low,
'Twas certain they called there so that one could go.

Scarce had the one that had been left all alone
Sipped once at her glass with her face like a stone,
Than light urgent feet in the passage were heard
And the other through the door flew out like a bird.
Both went up the road like two hares would in March,
And their glasses stood full and their throats were still parched,
And all the old rustics with winks watched them go
Through the big tavern window, where the lattice is low.

They chuckled and chaffed as the games took their course,
Some said 'could be better and some said 'could be worse.
Then the mystery unfolded to these who knew not
Why the dame who had entered flew out like a shot.
It seems that mine host kept an old breeding sow,
And sows with their noses are nosey enou',
And the sty where she rested was next to the place
From where many dames had left with much haste.

The old sow by her nosing had wrested away
The stone-work between them and there she would stay
So silent until she would hear someone move
Then loudly a grunt would that beldame remove.
It was worse for a stranger who knew not the place,
Nor what to expect when her presence did grace
The small moon-lit room out there in the yard
To flee it in terror from the coarse grunting bard.

But mine host was worried in case there should appear
A patron bereft of the sense of the ear,
Then the grunting old sow with her nose cold and hard
May well cost a life out there in the yard.
The story soon spread and the inn became known
As the one happy tavern where men keep alone.
For no matron it seems would risk losing her charms
Out there in the yard of the "Auctioneers Arms".

THE COLLIER

His day begins 'fore morning sky
Has driven night from way on high,
'Fore chanticleer has left his stall
To sound his morning clarion-call.

Aroused from slumber to the chair
Where busy housewife bustling there
Prepares his food before the fire
Tin-bonnet hiding plate and wire.

Soon hungry smells come from that spot
And fill each room of his small cot,
As crackling bacon spits and curls,
And steaming mug from spooning whirls.

His matron dressed for morning toil
Her clean bag-apron yet unsoiled
Cuts bread her careworn hands have made,
All oven-brown it stands displayed.

His meal is finished, on his feet
He draws his clogs steps to the street,
Calls out to some he cannot see
Tho' yet he hears their stride ring free.

He later finds his gall'ried room
And toils so hard in that black tomb;
A fleeting rest for 'snappin-bite'
Then work - where 'tis forever night.

Nor does he know while yet he toils
If death will stretch its lethal coils,
And crush or burn his mortal flesh,
Or poisoned air his lungs en-mesh.

When homely fires burn bright and warm
And flickering flames so shapely form,
Pray spare a thought for that black hole
And those whose life-blood wins the coal.

WISHES

Some will sigh for a tiny cot
Near where the breakers sound,
And find contentment is their lot
Where mighty waters pound.

And some there be whose joy is there
Where noise and walls entomb,
And chimneys stand so grey and bare
Like sentinels of doom.

Yet there be others seeking bliss
By roaming o'er the sea,
Each day a foreign dawn will kiss
The cheek of one so free.

And some are blest who roam the fell,
And tread the mossy dale,
To cull the wild flower in the dell,
And hear the song-birds tale.

Indeed, Man's blessings find no dearth,
To him a choice is given.
O'er all the creatures on this earth,
But he can make his heaven.

GARDENS

Walk the world of gardens
Flowers of every hue,
See them all in splendour
Waiting there for you.

Just beyond the window
Or the winding lane,
There they wait to greet you
Come, O come again.

By the pathways growing
In the hedgrows tall,
See them ere the winter
Spreads its deathly pall.

STAFFORDSHIRE

I've travelled the length of this country of ours
And some that lie over the main,
But the beauties I view seem to vanish like dew
At the mention of Staffordshire's name.

North Midlands and West is the place I love best,
Where moorlands stretch up to the blue,
By the Trent and the Dove lie the arbours of love,
What mem'ries fond they renew.

O sweet are the waters that Manifold pours,
The anglers delight in her sport,
While over the hills along Berrisford Dale,
What beauty there Nature has wrought.

By the south and the east where the grass grows the least
Dim factories stretch o'er the land,
Each playing its part in the fast beating heart
Of our dearly belov'ed England.

PARTING

Spring with wanton lust has greened the land
And blossoms hang so gaily on the tree;
The streams rush by the spot where hearts once sang
Where first you gave your precious love to me.

The tree emblazoned with a lover's sign
Cut deep the bark to last across the years,
Now fading 'neath the mosses, yours and mine,
A sight brings to my eyes the burning tears.

Sing minstrel, your nesting lover near,
Feel not the stinging barbs of humans frail,
For we love deep, and deeper yet the future fear,
Unseen events to come unknown, can make us quail.

THE ASHES or,
HOW MAN'S HAND IS STAYED IN
HIS PRIMARY QUEST FOR SELF-DESTRUCTION

When man with man will moil and bother
And seek to kill each one the other,
And ruin spreads its gory hands
Across the earth's most fertile lands,
And women weep in cheerless gloom
Upon a loved one's early tomb -
Across the world the glad news flashes
'England's brave sons have won The Ashes.'

The daggered hand restrains its thrust
'Fore sending flesh unto the dust,
The maddened, burning, leaden balls
Their humming death a moment stalls,
The murderous bomb from metalled bird
Restrains its screaming, now is heard
A sweeter note upon its breath -
Though at its end there still is death.

Some even view the tortured plain
And clasp their brother's hands again.
And through the haze of smoke and grime
They see a light begin to shine.
(A light that for too long was dim
When mortal man thought not on Him)
And unrestraining joy abounds
And hate and war find laurelled mounds.

A quizzic' look o'erspreads the face
Of those who are not of our race.
Confounded they because a sport
Can still the path that war has wrought,
Can make a nation quake with fear
When bat is taken cheap or dear;
A nation that its breath witholds
As windmilled arm so cleanly bowls.

Who sound a thunderous great applause
That easy drowns the guns of Mars,
When ball on peaceful mission flies
For six's bounds - or maybe five's.
Who never think it a disgrace
When care of beast takes pride of place
O'er that of child of tender years
Who's future holds such pain and fears.

Has this proud plot of island fame
Bred seperate men - without a name?
For none it seems are so complex,
We laugh at things that others vex,
And weep what they would laugh to scorn
And smile when riven by life's thorn.
We travel long with one that's strange
And never speak or glance exchange.

But, when freedom dies beyond the foam,
And persecution's wantons roam,
The victim of the Tyrant's hand
Turns eyes towards the promised land.
They come unhindered seeking rest
Unto these shores - a welcome guest,
To succour find and friendly hand
Here with thee, O fair England.

AROUND MORRIDGE

Such vistas grand ennoble this green shire,
From Ramshaw's pile it rolls and rolls
With scenes that never tire.
A'top high Morridge, crowned by heathers blaze,
The towering kestrel lifts to scan with piercing eye
The gently drifting haze.

Deep vallys green are cleft so steep below,
And there concealed from all and lying still
Is sheltered timid roe.
While hare and moorcock watch with 'magined fear,
As silent feet of stalking death pass by,
Now far - now ever near.

In remembrance soon a gentle journey make
And let minds eye wild wandering go
Again those paths to take,
To climb blue hills that boggy moorland hides
And turning, look down there-below
At Meerbrook's mirrored tides.

A tavern lone, with Mermaid's sportive sign,
Joins three long roads which touch the door,
Wind-worn, grey stones combine.
Such sights bring joy to those most needing rest,
For there a welcoming seat is found inside
A house so truly blest.

And lo! what views the broadest windows greet,
To see again that vast terrain
While taking ale and meat.
A severance found from life's dull-pathed routine,
To hear and see sweet nature's charms
Its varied brown and green.

ADONIS

His geneological tree doth run -
To Cinyras was born a son.
He grew to beauteous face and form
But from all love was kept forlorn.
He loved Diana's spear and bow
His hunting prowess he did show.

While yet unbearded he was seen
By Venus, of all Love the Queen.
And she desired the comely youth
To reach her end she tried forsooth.

She tried to gain him by her tears
But yet he pleaded tender years.
His roots were yet a budding green
Thro' portalled Love he ne'er had been.
Adonis left her fretting there
And those who saw did envious stare.

So to his hunting love went he
And killed he was, eventually.
A maddened boar with tusks that gleamed
His thigh and groin one day unseamed.
Poor Venus, quite distraught was she
And changed him to the anemone.
While Proserpine who saw it all
Adonis back to life did call.
He lived with her until each Fall
Then answered he Diana's call.

The anemone blooms in the leafy dell
Because in his youth sweet Adonis fell.
Had he not answered the hunting-call
That flower would ne'er have been at all.

HATTY

It must be over twenty years since Hatty, tragic died,
He is buried in the new church-yard over by the western side.
Some wealthy village gentleman his stone had ready bought,
For Hatty had made many friends 'fore Gabe his own had sought.
From where he lies you can see the pool and bridge without a rail,
And just beyond, the tavern where they sold the finest ale.

When he from mining trade had done, the parson, so sincere,
Had found light work for able hands the weeds from church-yard clear;
And trim the mounds, some very old and others sadly new,
And see the cuttings were all burned when they sheared the stately yew.
His stipend for these labours would, with pension, make a go,
For Hatty was a devout man - to blissful Barley-Mow -
And often after an evening bout with a flagon close at hand,
To himself he would talk by the ivied walk with the tombstones near at ha

By the church-yard wall was a sheltered bower where courting lovers sat
And whiled away the eventide, unfeared by owl or bat.
But sometimes when the moon was low and hanging by the ridge,
The eerie mumbling o'er the wall would make their spines go fridge.
Ungallantly then the youthful swain would take a hurried leave,
And the fearful maid would dab a tear with her starchy lace-frilled sleeve.
Then hurry down the shadowed lane and keep the centre-road,
While darting glances here and there as fear with reason strove.

Now Hatty hated owls and bats and things that move by night,
For ere he saw the light of day some thing had given fright.
So when from labour he was free a searching walk would take,
And clear the nest the owl had made and the batty perches shake.
But now he lies beneath his tomb that stands 'neath spreading yew,
Most every night the owls take flight and perch there two by two.
Right on the grave where Hatty lies they shower their proud disdain,
It took old Simon half a day to clear the stone of stain.

The stone was fashioned fancy-like with cross and circle too,
And the Muse had cut endearing lines in words so sad and true.
Old Simon would the mess clean up the owls had spread around,
But drew the line at batty slime that on the grave was found.
The parson gathered the flock around to see what they must do,
The problem was to move the grave or fell the stately yew.
Then like a ray of sunshine the answer it was found,
The spot where they had laid him was unconsecrated ground.
With due array and water the error was put right;
And ever since the marble stone has stayed a snowy-white.

'Twas in the pool by moonlight that Hatty sealed his fate,
And 'fore the stars had left the sky had reached the Golden Gate.
But how he came to be there was known but to a few,
And the more the village gossiped the more the mystery grew.
Till the parson said that his sad tale should now be fully told,
How for the drink he squandered all that he had to hold.
So that it may be a lesson taught to those who knew his fate,
And yet may change a wayward son before it was too late.
Mine host that night had left unlocked the door to cellared ale,
And dire thirst had led him there when the evening star grew pale.

Much later full of potent brew, he struggled to cross the pool,
But swaying, stepped from fenceless bridge and sank 'neath depths so cool.
Near by the pool at the unfenced bridge, a widow has her cot,
The woman heard a violent curse and to her window got
In time to see the bitter end the waste of an only man,
And she turned away with a bitter tear her lonely room to scan.
For Hatty it was found too late some female consorts had,
To each in turn he paid a call it all seemed rather sad
That all those maids would now bereft of little loving be,
And never know again the thrill of his long and bony knee,
Nor taste again the hairy lip that soaked the barley-brew,
Nor smell the coat so worn and soiled that served his bed-couch too.

Around the pool some moonlight night his ghost is often seen,
And his voice still heard o'er the church-yard wall where lovers sit and dream
Fond hands place flowers in sweet array where his mouldering bones do lie,
And still some women speak his name with a dreamy wistful sigh.
It matters not where he is now for clothes or even ale,
So let him be - God rest his soul - and so ends Hatty's tale.

TO....................

The moon is hinging in the trees
The blossoms hing upon the bough;
The world has spun round three or four
I think I'll see her now.

No light is shining from her room
The curtains tell the open door.
I'll wager she has ta'en the bridge
Where Blythe's sweet waters pour.

My feet go winging o'er the moor,
The silent turfs their secrets keep,
My arms now clasp her tiny waist
While all the world is wrapt in sleep.

A SOLDIER *(Found dead - 1944*
in France. (German)

Symbolic of thy Maker's work
(In which 'tis said His like may lurk)
The parchment skin and eyeless gaze
With sagging jawbone mark amaze.

O mortal brother freed from hell,
Encamped in this hot stinking cell,
A nauseous sight to say the least,
Where bussing blow-flies find a feast.

And yet - my thoughts so solemn take
A winging flight beyond your wake -
To home, for young you were for sure
Ere call to arms came to your door.

A strutting, murdering, jackboot Hun?
Ah no! a misled, fearful mother's son;
Alas, like me in war enmeshed
To satisfy some selfish quest.

THE ANGLERS

When dawn has filled the sky
And brids begin to fly,
With rod and line and fly
They angle Dove.
While stretched on mossy banks they spy
Blue skies above.

Where stilly pools lie deep
And nodding aspens weep,
There on the banks they creep
'Midst noisy weir,
And watch the beauties glide and leap
In waters clear.

The line-tipped lucious May
Was hatched that very day.
A snick, a bending and then play
The gamely trout,
In flight he zooms so far away
Then turns about.

The landing net submerge
Nearby the grassy verge,
While watching every violent surge
With venerate eyes,
Then on the bank the final dirge
For glis'ning prize.

I WALKED ONE DAY WHERE
FLOWERS WERE BLOOMING

I walked one day where flowers were blooming,
Blooming gaily down the lane,
Where purple lilacs were perfuming
And coverts sang their loud refrain.
Each tiny throat poured out its blessing,
Blessing all who saw and heard,
Each flower and spray the zephyr's pressing
And mingled were the scents it stirred.

I thought again of those then toiling,
Toiling sweating 'neath the ground,
In their gall'ries, wretched moiling,
Even then would they be found.
That thought so black my mind was clouding,
Clouding, dark'ning all my sight,
Soon that tomb around me shrouding
Where 'tis forever always night.

I clutched a flower that bloomed so tender,
Tender flowerlet on the spray,
The hidden thorn did pain engender,
The rose's petals fell away.
A moment's joy was all their living,
Then they fluttered to the ground,
Like the pleasures life is giving,
A moment gone - ne'er to be found.

ON A RELUCTANT..........

The gurgling stream its music lends
As weaving on its way it wends,
Each tree in nodding rhythm bends
To native charm,
Yet as my eyes love's message sends
You show alarm.

Has no-one breached those fiery lips?
Has no-one touched those moulded hips?
Or passing glanced those sculptured tips
That firm each breast?
O passion's dagger, how it rips
The wooer's chest.

A maid ne'er was for viewing sent,
Nor just for loving e'er was lent
But man all ways is ever sent
On fruitless quest
But one thing foremost 's been his bent -
'Tis yet his best.

Our Maker's wisdom we acclaim,
In book and praise we sing his name
King Solomon did ne'er disdain
To follow thus,
And multiply across earth's plain
His thousands - plus!

THE MANIFOLD

Tall and stately Morridge stands
With crown of rocky heath,
While from her bosom springs Manifold
Like a silvery ribboned wraith.

She pours across the peaty moors
And down to meet the lea;
More greener vales now welcome her
As she journey's through Throwley.

Then on to stony Ilam's place
To form a pretty pool
Where speckled sport choose reedy side
'Neath aspen tree so cool.

A pause then on again so swift,
To Ilam's Cross goodbye,
Okeover Hall in meadow stands
Where borders meet nearby.

She joins her sister gentle Dove
To journey to the Trent,
Forever leaves the sweet brown hills
Where her brief youth was spent.

Fair thee well, sweet Manifold,
Your fate now seems unfair
Ere long your broad and crystal stream
A darker tinge to share.

THE TRIAL

On trial stood the inglorious three
Who on the earth lived sinfully.
"And what have you to say to me?"
Said Nick with scorn,
And gloomily they fixed his e'e
And pointed horn.

The first one spake and wheedling tones
Marked well the voice of lying Jones,
He pleaded for his worthless bones,
Lies flowed with ease,
He 'viegled Nick with tears and moans
That seemed to please.

"I really don't know why I'm here",
Lied he with voice that quaked with fear,
"No wrong I've done - ne'er tasted beer,
Nor sinful love."
"I know full well why you're sent here."
Nick did reprove.

The devil's tail twitched to and fro,
His eyes like fires began to glow
And on poor Jones they did bestow
Their fullest glare,
"You've lied to me - you're doomed you know
How could you dare?".

And silent fell the devil then
As human voice was heard again.
I'm Creepa, and I'm sure my frien',
You are mistaken,
It's I that should be in Heaven,
Not here - forsaken. -

I must have missed the heavenly way
As we came here the other day
So back I'll go, don't keep my pray,"
He said so boldly,
Tho' on his face pale fear there lay
In marks so coldly.

Seth Roper spoke with a lowered head
"I've often cursed - had sinful bed
And known the end would see me led
Thro' thy hot ovens.
I'm pleased to meet you, Nick," he said,
"And all my cousins".

"Now hold!" said Nick. "Before you go
I'll let you see your past on show."
He watched their faces redder glow
More than his fire,
'Twas plain to see like taughtened bow
Had grown his ire.

He scratched his chin then turned and spake
To the horn'ed host there at his wake.
"The first two there to the burning stake."
And when they'd gone
He turned to Seth his hand did shake,
"O like you, son."-

But hold!" he said and danced with glee
"We'll watch those two burn merrily."
Seth had no choice but to agree
To Nick's proposal.
Then off they went on some mad spree
And gay carousal.

ANNIE

Come sit a'side o' me, Annie,
And hing your lips on mine,
And tell me of some future bliss
We'll share-just yours and mine.
And I will hold you fast, my love,
We'll gaze up at the sky,
And pledge each wondrous whispered word
While shafts flit o'er the sky.

I'll tell you this as well, my love,
No peace have I alone,
The chanting brids, the woodlark's song,
The floods that leap the stone,
All fall neglected on my sight -
They once would stay my tread -
Until you say that you'll be mine,
Such joys for me are dead.

O, COME WITH ME

O come with me, O come with me
Across the fields so fair,
And I will make a daisy chain
To crown your sunny hair.
The gold-cup flower I'll cull and touch
Unto your neck so white,
We'll walk together by the stream
Where fishes gleam so bright.

O come with me, O come with me,
Where pearly grasses shine,
They hang upon each gilded stem
And all are yours and mine.
But let the sunrise touch each orb
Before you clutch it near,
And gold is there within your sight
All, all for you my dear.

O come with me, O come with me,
Where nature has her store,
Where minstrels play and sing their tune
And murmuring waters pour.
All these my love with pleasure find,
Are set for our delight,
So come with me, O come with me,
And stay - my love requite.

THE YOUNG COLLIER

The early sun may kiss our brow
Before we go below,
And patriot fervours tell us how
And where and when to go;
Exploited by great cent per cent
And those that hold the coin,
Who little give for mighty stent -
Who our brief lives purloin.
When will it end? the bodies cry
That sweat and toil in pain,
Whose narrow birth and shallow life
Know naught but shackling chain.

173

CONVERSATION OVERHEARD
BETWEEN AN OLD MAN AND
SOME BOYS ON AN OMNIBUS

I see you gaze
With deep amaze
At my red nasal-organ,
And pass remarks about cabbage-stalks
And things that cause ovation.
Had your parents, boy,
Spent as much employ
Upon your education,
As it cost to place
This on my face,
Which I hold in veneration,
You would not be
So rude to me,
And speak with degradation
About my nose -
Which lovely glows,
My pride - and my creation!

SPRING

The snow has gone from the moorland,
Wild turfs are heaving green,
And minstrels vie twixt hedge and sky
To tune their throats so keen.

The hazel waves her dark catkins
The streams go rushing by,
And nature's children flit in pairs
And ours are wondering why.

And frocks made up last summer
An azure sky brings forth,
All ironed anew - the maiden wears -
Despite blasts from the north.

The lane has saved her fresh hawthorn
For that first loving pair,
And mavis, topmost on the bough,
Her greeting gives from there.

STEPPING STONES, DOVEDALE

What timeless feet have braved the surge
And crossed the Dove's wild restless urge.
Clip-clopped their way without a fear
From stone to stone symmetric clear.

Young love's join hands to leap entwined,
While aged more slow a resting find.
So youthful fly the leaping feet
And bound to music's tuneful beat.

An artist's brush you have enslaved,
While exiles have your likeness craved.
Nostalgia comes with tears and moans
At sight of Dovedale's stepping stones.

THE FOX

He walks at dawn when dew has kissed the grass
And soft as mists his footfalls slowly pass.
Across the lane, nose in the air he moves,
But now and then will leap where deep lie cartwheel grooves.

He'll stop, and every nerve a'kindle, stare
At something ahead, unseen - but there;
His every fibre taut, his nose a'twitch,
His eyes unblinking gaze along the dripping ditch.

Slowly, slowly his belly sinks to earth,
An instinctive move implanted there from birth.
Concealed, intent, his eyes now mouldering fire,
Neck hair erect, fangs slowly bared he feels a growing ire.

Motionless, then slowly upwards raise,
A bound, a leap then into the morning haze.
A frightful squeal then silence once again
As burdened with his prey he leaves the misty lane.

TO MY LOVE

The morn has kissed the mountain stream
The dew has kissed the rose,
The woodbine twines around its beam
Where linnets find repose.
Soft blows the bluebells, fragrant there,
As bends each leafy bough
Where happy minstrels seek the air
To pledge their tuneful vow.

O' can my love be slumbering still,
'Midst these affections rest?
Or does the grinding, aching mill
Of love not know her breast?
The thought as quick came to my mind
Was gone - ne'er to return,
For by the window's coloured blind
Stands she for whom I yearn.

Yet but a moment in my arms
Your cheek pressed close to mine,
To lingering savour all your charms
While yet there is but time.
The miser with his golden hoard,
The king o'er his domain,
The rarest gem torn from this earth
For you would I disdain.

MORNING

How peaceful are the rural scenes
On a summer morn,
When gossamers hang from the leafy beams
At dewy dawn,
And the blue wood smoke curls up so straight
From the chimney snug;
And the yeoman leans at the five-barred gate
Where the briars tug.
When the tiny swift finds an early wing
Beneath the thatch;
To the twittering brood that is clamouring
It wings its catch;
And the goslings proudly follow their dam
To the muddy pool,
And cow-house doors begin to slam
Behind milking-stool;
And the word that was sung at an earlier time
By clarion-call,
Brings forth with joy the pleasant rhyme
That is made by all.

LINES....ON THE PROSPECT
OF PARENTHOOD

O come when frosts lie on the fells
Or white with blanket snow,
A welcome here's awaiting thee
And such a royal show.

O come with summer's happy time
Or ripe with rosy June,
When thorny blossoms scent the air
And hedgerows hum their tune.

O come with autumn's golden store
Or winter's blasts so cold,
Just suit thyself, my joy to be,
Thou'rt welcome more than gold.

TO THE EXCHEQUER

Come weep with me my honest friends
The world's against us it never mends,
And now th' Exchequer's joined the war
And drove his knife to take our gore.
The thieving rascal's venting spite
From lowly poor takes venomed bite
And priced beyond our feathered purse
Our bit of joy - on him a curse!
Justice, friends, has left our shore,
Next year, mayhap, 'twill cost us more,
While those who drink the foreign wine
(That makes their noses bloom and shine)
Just pay the same from year to year
While each new budget costs us dear.
His honeyed promise "Fair for all"
Will make the honest christian pall,
And while he glibly coins the phrase
And leads us in politic maze
He slaps the tariff on our ale,
To pay for nuts and ships for whale!

THE CYNIC

Who scoffs at Freedom let him see
The bloody page of History.
Who ne'er enslaved can ever be
Will scarce rejoice at Liberty.
Know not a pang in hunger's name,
Feel nothing for the beggar's claim.

Take shares for two for one to live
Then yet for one there's none to give.
Should strength conjoin a tyrant's name
Then terror will the weaker claim.
The heavier there a place will find
Where weakest link will soon unbind.

If Power finds a mind that's small
Then woes on minions heavy fall.
Officials, Statutes cry Nay! Nay!
A purse will change them to Yea! Yea!.
Their praise to God they loudly shout
So long as God from them takes nowt'.

DAWNING

Beauteous stranger from the east
Thy coming brings a vision's feast,
Once so red presaging gloom,
Another bright from azured broom.
And yet another grey fortells,
As clouds and mists haste o'er the fells.

Thy kiss awakes the budding rose,
Thy fingers touch each flower that grows,
And on each lacy branch of spring
Thy heralds mount and sweetly sing.

Thy welcome face is gladly seen
To signal songs around the green.
Still many toil upon thy bell
While others find their earthly cell.

Prolific pens to thee have sung,
For thee oftimes the bells have rung,
And grateful eyes have turned to thee
And thanks evoked-for leave to see.

EVENTIDE

How lovely is the eventide
When skies are all aglow,
With tints of crimson flecked with gold
That shepherd love and know.

When hushed are coverts of their song
And kine are lowing home,
And round the pens the gadwing flies
To hum his ceaseless drone.

When mists fall light on stilly pools
And cornfields fallow lie
While o'er its bosom brown and bare
The timid hares go by.

FEBRUARY

See how restless grows the river
Darkened by alluvial yest;
Carried by the new-born streamlets
To the parent river's breast.

Rush the pregnant turgid waters
Boiling frothing spume is blown;
Surging round the willowed 'bankment
Leaving roots bereft of loam.

Beside the river lying low there
Pastures yet untouched by beast.
Overnight become a lakeland
The gourmand river takes its feast.

O'er its guiding channels leaping
Spreading out across the plain,
Searching in each nook and cranny,
Tyrant of the sprouting grain.

Bereaved and homeless scrawls the brown-shrew
To the hedgerow's leafy floor;
Driven from his snugly burrow
Never to return there more.

Now the north wind fans the river
O'er the pools blows icy air,
Frosty fern-like patterns forming
On the surface water there.

The sea-gulls wheel and take their pleasure
On the glassy surfaced pools;
Shunning they the raging sea-shore
Till the ocean's temper cools.

Nature's times and laws bewilder us,
Made and known by One alone;
Method's there though man's eyes see none,
And all must His great wisdom own.

MARCH

This the month of sprouting green
Boxing hare and winds so keen
That blustering keep the skyways clear,
And lanes are dry with dust so dear.

The ploughman follows the furrowing team,
The ploughshare soon takes silvery gleam.
And greedy gulls drives lesser fry
With raucous cries into the sky.

The lark above so sweetly sings
The airy notes that tell of Spring.
While meadow green his mate conceals,
His song to her his love reveals.

The bare-worn hill will now disclose
A secret kept beneath the snows;
Where dormouse had his humble room
And slept away dull Winter's gloom.

Through woodland carpet - yet so bare -
Narcissi peep and take the air;
And crocus brings to mossy dells
The earliest art of Nature's spells.

The budding grove with song is filled
By blackbird; thrush and chaffinch billed.
While from his bourne by oaken root
Old reynard lopes with wary foot.

The foamy, babbling, gurgling rill
O'erfed beyond its bounds will spill,
And work amongst the reedy turf
There leave the hopping spawners berth.

Can Man's creations e're replace
The timeless art of Nature's face?
That changes with each seasonal hour
From snowy gloom to leafy bower.

SPRINGTIME

The crocus rears its tiny head
Above the earth's brown sward,
While rivulets to torrents grown,
Leap o'er the stony ford.
An early bite is now revealed
Aneath some sheltered glade
And lambkins frolic filled with joy
As early spring's displayed.

With earnest flight the rooky pair
Go searching to the wood,
While magpies thatch their dome with care
And moorhens risk the flood.
Much-loved, respected, robin's breast
Aflame for all to see,
He'll build his home in some tin-can,
Or some bit holly tree.

The woodland from a mass of brown
O'ernight may change to green,
As dormant buds may shily peep
'Midst air that's bright and keen.
Where eddied pools reflect the sky
The aspen's mirrored there,
And catkins gently sway their scent
O'er bees that forage there.

MAY-DAY

Eager eyes will look at dawning
View the light of coming day,
Watch the sky lest dark clouds forming
Mar this birth of glorious May.
Maidens dresses gay with flowers,
Donned again for any flaw,
'Fore they step from cottage bowers
To the soft green grassy floor.

Doting eyes will watch their tresses,
Bows and ribbons set so fair,
As the maidens dance their dresses
Float like goss'mer on the air.
Fiddles playing loud and clearly
Start the covert into song,
Brock will yawn and stretch so dreary
Wakened all the dormered throng.

Youthful feet beat tireless rhythm
Silently upon the sward,
Age reclines but nods it with them,
Rooks in chorus sound their chord.
Now the moment is approaching
When the May Queen will be crowned,
All around her throne encroaching
See her beauty far renowned.

Regaled she sits in all her splendour,
Crowned her hand the sceptre holds,
Gasps from all her looks engender,
Flashing eyes her smile embolds.
Enthroned so proud she looks and queenly,
Fussing matrons smooth her dress,
The queens uncrowned pay homage seemly
And wish the new sweet happiness.

The parson's words respectfully follow,
And thankful hearts there will evoke,
A prayer that rural charms unfallow,
Be ever free of urban yoke.
The games and frolics in their courses
Gambol gaily o'er the green,
Gladdened hearts seen there endorses,
Simple arts remain supreme.

The cooling day draws to its closing
And tiredly they leave the scene,
Flushed with joy to sweet reposing
Full their glorious day has been.
The womenfolk sit by their cottage,
Talking happy of the day,
The stranger tall who tossed the forage,
The dresses worn so fine and gay.

The men-folk each his own way starting
Where the tavern sign is seen,
To hear the bard his lay imparting
All the joys that mind may ween.
So night with softened air and smiling,
Falls so gently o'er the scene,
Where lingering lovers hours beguiling,
Ere disclosed by heavenly queen.

Some choose the seat 'neath thorny bowers
Where the blossom scents the air,
Limpid now the garland-flowers
Round the maiden's lovely hair.
Now they clasp and kiss so lingering
Slowly then wend on their way,
Each this moment long remembering -
Their love so young, and May.

ON SEEING A CUCKOO PURSUED BY BIRDS.

I wonder why they're chasing thee
With angered haste, persistently.
Did'st find a nest in some bit tree
To spawn
That was not thine, now yet was free
To own?

And did some minstrel from the glen
Cry, "Thief" and "Shame", ag'en, ag'en,
And did they all surround thee then
With ire,
And chase thee from that tiny den
Like fire?

O speckled stranger when I look
And see thee blot thy spotless book
By cheating robin, dunnock, rook
Then flee,
In shame I cast a downward look
For thee.

With happy hearts we hear thy call
So pleased our woods are yet thy stall,
Yet vain thou giv'st thy name to all
Thy sound,
And stay so brief - until the fall
Comes round.

There's no forgiving acts like thine,
No brid can say "This fledgeling's mine",
Yet will it stodge like any swine
Can do,
And all his voice when grown so fine
'S, "Cu-ckoo!"

I wonder now O sorry bird,
Who in thy mind this evil stirred,
And if some human act or word
Was known
To change thee to what they prefered
Alone.

Or did'st when flying on thy round
Hear some unfaithful word or sound,
And looking, saw them there aground
With joy,
(Some other's mate, I will be bound)
And coy.

For it is known the human nest
Has known and reared a foreign crest,
So it would seem my voice had best
Be quiet,
For yet to speak may cause unrest -
Or riot.

TO JULIE

When I see a sunny day,
When gentle breezes dance and play,
When I smell the scented may
I shall think on Julie.

As each morning fills the sky
Her vision first shall fill my eye,
'Tis then I'll heave a wistful sigh
And think of you, sweet Julie.

THE LOVE THAT YOU AWAKENED

The love that you awakened
Like the morning fades away,
As dew on flowers
Will vanish with the day.

Your heart some new one favours,
To your falsehood it attends
Love's fortune waiting,
To late enmeshed it rends.

Then barbs all life destroying -
Run fast, O heart, away -
Lest you, regretting,
The tearful price must pay.

KATHY'S COTTAGE

Her tiny home's within the square
Of mellowed stone and grey,
Where chestnuts spread their shadows wide
When summer fills the day.
Around the door the woodbine twines
And roses 'neath the sill,
The evening stock with might zest
Their scent the nightimes fill.

The shining windows bright and neat
With ribboned curtains hung.
The lattice up above hangs wide
Where martins nests are strung
The twittering broods and wings that hum
Bring to her lips a smile,
And when morning sounds awake the air
Her songs will all beguile.

How oft I've stood beneath that thatch
With youth's mad racing heart
That stopped at every clicking latch
Which pierced like any dart.
Her soft footfall her warm embrace
Then haste where shadows fall,
To realise love's blissfull dreams
Beside the churchyard wall.

O DO YOU REMEMBER?

Remember, O do you remember
The nights of our delight?
When whispering music filled the air
So far into the night.
The gentleness of love we gave,
The kisses soft and warm,
The sweet caress, the fond embrace
That made my pulses storm -
Remember, O do you remember?

FAREWELL

Must this be our fond farewell
Must we ever strangers be,
Must I take the road forgetting
What you'll ever mean to me.

Must those mem'ries born of gladness
Loving moments we've embraced,
Come to naught be ever silent,
Barren like a desert waste.

Life its precious moments fleeting
Hastes so soon to age and fears,
Let us give new love a greeting
Youth and pleasure know not tears.

MY SALLY O

When o'er the rolling fields I stray
While brids are warbling happy O,
I cannot hear their cheering songs
For thinking of my Sally O.

I cross the rushing bounding stream,
Where fishes sport so merry O,
I miss their flashing silvery gleam
When thinking on my Sally O.

The woodland breezes sing their song
Among the branches hanging low,
I cannot smell the scented may
For thinking on my Sally O.

While looking for her lovely form
The minutes wing so painful slow,
My heart's near breaking standing here
Just waiting for my Sally O.

For her I'd scale the greatest height
I'd plumb the ocean's depths so low,
I'd face the devil's awful might
And more, for my dear Sally O.

O HAPPY THE MAN

O happy the man with a home full of bliss
And children from one to a score,
Whose met at the door with a smile and a kiss
And tiny feet pattering the floor.

Who toils through the day for his eventide rest
And the fire blazing bright in the grate,
Who watches with joy o'er his brood and his nest
Content with his fortune, and fate.

Tho' the world judge him poor by their standards of wealth
He is rich in the true love he shares,
His stride on through life is devoid of all stealth,
Tho' its burden of sorrows he shares.

BY THE OLD BRIDGE

O! meet me by the old bridge, Maggie,
While the moon is shining bright,
Where the water's still and silent
Here my heartbeat fill the night.

By the streamlet, waves the blossom,
And the flowerlets on each spray,
Scents so rich the air perfuming
While the moon makes night as day.

Take my hand and feel its tremble
Like the leaves on aspen bough,
What is life without a lover?
Naught would I exchange for now.

Tell me once again you love me
While my arms enfold you tight,
While our lips caress each other
Like the gentle breeze at night.

As a King o'er his dominions
Rules sweet love o'er mine and thine,
Filling each bright hour with pleasures
Eyes like jewels lips like wine.

O! meet me by the old bridge, Maggie,
See the moon is shing bright,
Let us haste and find seclusion
In the silence of the night.

THE TALE OF THE DOVE

Where gentle Dove flows soft and clear
Her murmerings tell a tale so dear,
How sweet Narcissus found her stream
To rest, and of his Echo dream.

He saw his features mirrored there
In limpid water soft and fair,
And enamoured with what he saw
Forgot he then his Echo more.
But she poor nymph can still be heard
When Dovedale sounds the calling bird.

Those waters same speak Leda's name,
When she caused Jupiter heart-bane,
He saw her graceful heavenly form
Into the waters gently born.
So he took on the shape of swan
And won her to beget Helen.

They also tell to those who hear
How Bacchus past the waters near
And, charmed by beauty all around
Caused wine to flow up from the ground.

An so Apollo blessed the dale
Where sunlight's smile doth never fail
And nymphs foregathered by the Dove
And named the place, 'The Vale of Love'.

THE CHANGING SCENE

A time there was when England's poor
Whose terraced cots stood door to door
Dependent were on neighbours good,
And lived as all good neighbours should,
When food was scarce and clothes were thin
And leaky roofs let winter in
And Christmas was another day,
Nought could that cheerful band dismay.
And yet though poverty was theirs
They richer far beyond compare,
For they found happiness within
That wealth destroys and makes a sin.
Evil desires and pompous pride
Could never trammel their stalwart stride,
As in their chapels in every street
They taught the child of Jesu's sweet.
When careworn wife felt pangs of birth
Of neighbours help there was no dearth.
One fetched the babe with expert care -
No midwife or a doctor there -
Another took the children in
And fed and washed looked after them.
Another cleaned each room and sill
And came again while wife was ill.
Though life was hard it left no stain
To mar the joy or quell the pain,
Life was accepted with its load,
They pawns of wealth and power that strove.
When calls to arms were bugled then
Their praise was far beyond all ken.
And they crossed foreign soil and sea
And kept these shores of tyrants free.

But free for what? to starve in shame
And find a grave without a name?
While those who wield politic power
See their estate grow hour by hour.
How rich the poor in goodness then,
How ill exchanged is now for then
For gone it seems is the helping hand
As independent now they stand,
Pretending wealth and false with pride
Before real poverty with them has died.
The chapels that their parents knew
With echoes tell the empty pew.
The simple train who found easy joy
And blushed with ease of nature coy,
Now show a mean and hardened face
That once was meek with kindly grace.
A selfishness reserved for wealth
Creeps through the land with cruel stealth,
Providing means for sensual pleasure
And taking that which man should treasure.
The Science climbs with knowledge rare
Sees some of Nature's secrets bare
And proudly boasts power Infinite,
O'er Universe they spread their might.
But one day this mad flight will end
For mightiest God is still man's friend.

LINES . . . . WRITTEN AT SLEDMERE

Spring is here ere elsewhere in the land,
The trees are gay umbrageous, and flowers on every hand.
White candle-blossom the chestnuts wave blue jasmine's hangs down
The rowans wave their snowy heads near hawthorn's milky crown.
The feathered minstrels mount the lofty boughs
And to some love sing out their heartfelt vows.

Around the Hall far-stretched is all of green,
Landscaped, so breathless is the view that wandering eyes have seen
Majestically, the stone fair wrought the centuries have touched fair,
And though there's grandeour man has made it's homely-warm in there
For England's past is felt and seen by all the things displayed,
And having seen a breed as this her future's not dismayed.

Each tiny cottage with garden set so neat,
The village school, the green and there the welcome seat.
And lone old 'Triton' lines the clustered way
To offer sustenance and charm to all who care to stay.
O smiling Sledmere! retain your peace and calm,
And may Saint Thomas ever watchful, protect you from all harm.

O tend your monolith with its graphic tale,
How from your yeoman's hand the Hun was want to quail
And when the fight was o'er and won to peaceful arts again,
To yolk the pair a'fore the plough and seed the fruitful plain.
O keep these things for England's good
And you'll be blest - as blest are all things good.

THE ROSE

No special hue but colours rare
The meanest plot will show so fair
In wild abandon growing there,
Your slaves observe,
And yet can only stand and stare
With mild reserve.

My country hails thee as its flower,
A maiden's blush thy petalled bower,
O'er love and heart thou art the power,
The mystic charm,
Such beauty knows no prisoning tower
But loving arm.

When all the leaves have blown away
And grasses green have shunned the day
And winter comes to wield his sway,
Thou'rt shining there
To hold fair summer's foes at bay,
Alone and bare.

In spring thy rosy buds break green
While yet the frosts are biting keen,
While yet the snowdrops there are seen
In bright array,
'Midst air so bright and crystal clean
You hail the day.

O' rose the summer is thy time
No fragrance yet compares to thine,
It hangs so heavy and like wine
Our senses take,
But yet for thee the heart doth pine
When thoughts awake.

ON FINDING A RABBIT ALIVE
IN A SNARE.

What sight I see beside the gorse,
Such visions fill me with remorse
When harmless creatures feel the force
Of cruel man,
Whose followed true his hellish cause
Since time began.

Was it perhaps upon your run
You bounded on so full of fun,
Or, maybe running from the gun
The noose snicked tight,
And there you lay while twice the sun
Gave way to night.

The more you pulled that murderous thong
The tighter round your neck it strung
Till weak, half dead, you lay among
The dewy grass,
To gasp some air into your lung
Where it will pass.

See now the snare is ripped away,
You'll live to run another day
And gambol o'er the clovered lay
In happy frolic,
Now "Look before you leap" they say,
Is friendly logic.

A snare awaits us all I fear,
No matter how we careful steer,
And tho' ahead we deign to peer
The present traps us,
Then late, too late the path is clear
As death enwraps us.

So brother mortal, to your home,
You're snug beneath the sandy loam,
No debts, no cares around your nome,
Nor brain to reason,
Nor need you toil for food nor roam
Far from your besom.

BRIGAND

*Being the tale of a Beagle, member
of the North Staffs. Moorland pack
who persistently absented himself
there-from during the chase. This
being a plea for his life against the
order that he should be put down....*

The case before you now concerns
The life of one who broke his terms.
Quite briefly now I will explain -
And this I do with heartfelt pain -
Just why before you for his life
Stands Brigand, of offences rife!

The pack was hunting near Throwley
And e'er anon they ran full free,
Each giving tongue and bounding on
It scarely seemed the day had gone.
When Elliott stood with eagle eye
And counted them as they went by,
Although the missing numbered six,
Five later found - of Brigand, nix!
And wearied all with ne'er a catch
The hounds recalled so well the match.
Then homeward to their kennels bent,
For Brigand on the searchers went
Until the darkness finalled day
And muttering threats each went his way.

Now let us turn as soon must we,
Review his plea of 'Not Guilty',
Were he as able for to talk
As well he does from duty walk,
I think mayhap he may say thus,
That he likes not such ones as us.
But I insist he has no choice
To pick and choose and whims to voice.
He's kept and fed and trained to be
A servant to our sport - not free!

It seems that when the pack gave voice
And entered woodland of their choice,
That dastard Brigand spied his chance
And sidled off with scarce a glance.
A farm nearby of goodly size
Contained the all of Brigand's eyes;
A lissome creature black and white
And lively as an elfin sprite.
Her dam a collie, tender, true,
Her sire his parentage ne'er knew.

The youngest time of any year
Doth not alone the human stir,
All nature feels the surging blood,
The high and low - the bad and good.
And why should Man disdainful be
When canine heart runs blithly free?
'Twas her first season yet unspoiled,
Her hot young blood for days had boiled.
And there this canine beauty stood
To tempt, enchant as females would.

To her flew Brigand panting hard
But not with toil upon the sward,
He captured her and took the prize
While timid hearts and envious eyes
Surveyed the scene, but would not broach,
Nor on his pleasure durst encroach,
His fangs were bared to fight for love
And win the favours of his dove.

When Phoebus in his glory rose
And touched the peaks with liquid gold
Pert Brigand knew a shackling-chain
That made his proud heart pump with pain.
And here he stands and pleads for life,
He states that all things take a wife.
A teardrop falls from his brown eyes
(As brown as the heath o'er which he flies)
And I in turn must add my plea
And ask that Brigand be set free.
'Tis hard for Man to scorn free love
Against it all have sometime strove.
Can we expect a canine heart
To share the morals we impart?
A heart whose love ne'er knows no bouds
For Master, Man or even hounds.

ON SEEING THE MANGLED FORM
OF AN HARE TORN BY HOUNDS

Poor wretch that it should be your lot
To live 'longside of man
Whose ne'er content with what he's got
But grasps on either han'.
The mangled bits of fur and bone
All scattered here and there,
Have drawn from me full many a moan
That some I know will share.

What sight to see you in the field
At dawn or close of day,
Your turn and speed the only shield
Till hounds have you at bay.
Amid some reeds she waits in vain
With down still at her breast,
For you poor wretch were born to be
A sport that cowards quest.

I know your form is near the brook
Beneath the willow's shade,
I promise there I'll often look
Until your debt is paid.
A bit of parsley there she'll find,
And fruits in season too,
And unto all your kith and kind
I'll find for winter through.

YE MAIDENS

O maidens I beg you pray heed this advice
When a passionate love you resist,
'Tis better to live with regret for a sin
Than regret, when too late what you've missed.

ON BEING INTRODUCED TO THE
MAYOR-ELECT IN A TAVERN
TOILET.

I scarce had time to be alone
When down my heart sank like a stone;
Within that place men call their own
The two stood there,
A lettuce-hand to me was thrown
More'n I could bear.

"I'd like you now to meet my friend"
Said he and from his waist did bend.
"A better man we ne'er can send
To be our Mayor",
(I thought 'tis for himself he'll fend
Once in that chair).

I made the usual p'lite remark
And watched their faces grow so dark,
"I'm sure," said I, "He'll make his mark
Upon finances,
He'll break the Bench, and then the Clerk
If given the chances -

But should he not some other will,
We must accept that bitter pill."
Their mouths agape they stood stockstill,
Their eyes did glare,
"The place we're in it comes not ill
To meet a Mayor".

DAY'S ENDING

I'll hasten now my toil is done
To where the fire burns red,
As red it burns like setting sun
When daylight's weary shed.
And she will meet me by the gate
With parted lips of love,
To clasp her near I ne'er can wait
For she's my only dove.

Her face upturns and mirrored there
I see the goodly light,
There's none so sweet nor yet so fair,
Naught can her eye outbright.
The glory of sweet heavenly bliss
Is mine to have and hold,
And where is apple-smell I'll kiss,
With joy my arms enfold.

Let others take their earthly wealth
With gems and gold to crown,
I'll take the precious gift of health
And love that leaves no frown.
With her my evenings wing their way
And soon 'tis morning bright,
And then we'll part until the day
Once more enjoins the night.

The trials that the day has brought
Her love uplifts with ease,
Supplanting each with happy thought
Like summer-wakened trees.
And so 'twill be until the end
When each and all must part,
For to His will all things must bend -
E'en love is torn apart.

THOSE MOSSY BANKS

I stood on Dove's green mossy banks
Ere morn had filled the sky.
I saw the mists unfold their view
To Tissington on high.
The gentle waters softly sang
'Fore lark had lifted there,
Nor stirred the blossoms where they hang
In that sweet vale so fair.

When dawn at last came o'er the hill
And touched the Spires with red,
Sweet Nature waked from drowsy sleep,
And minstrels left their bed.
Each mounted on some flowery stem
And vied with notes so grand,
O surely there's no other place
Like this in fair England.

The hills resounded with their song
As warming rays came down
And pointed out each dewy pearl
That studded nature's gown.
Each flowerlet there so gaily dressed
Had opened to the day,
And insects hummed their busy quest
To labour while they may.

That gentle lift of spiral blue
Marks Ilam in the glade.
Where Bertram, Saint of Blessed name,
Last battled with the Shade.
Now on his bridge that spans the weir
So many pledge their love,
While silver water glides beneath
And smiles at them above.

The years have marked each stony cross
That in the churchyard stands,
And safe within each hallowed spot
They lie with crossed hands.
But older still - the mellowed stone
Around the archway door,
And grooved and worn by countless feet
The aisleways cross the floor.

How many pilgrims here have knelt?
How many more to be?
How often has the sceptic laughed
To later bend a knee?
How many maidens kneeling there
With eyes upturned and wide,
Have dropped a tear and wistful prayer
For that white veil and bride?.

O places yet so dear to me
By Nature rich endowed,
I tremble for your future fate
And masters rich and proud.
Who yet may sweep your mark away
And beauties fair purloin,
And rip the seam twixt God and Man
For sake of golden coin.

THE JARROW MARCHERS

In streets where dimly houses stand
To mock a great and fearless band,
There lives so poor that valiant seed
Whom history marks of greatest deed.
Who far beyond the raging main
Have nations quelled for England's fame,
And tyrants quaked on bloody throne
When her navies thundered o'er the foam.
And those same men their duty done
Returned to show how fame was won.
But ere the sun had set its flame
Forgotten were their deed and fame.

They march in hunger from the north -
They only ask for bread and work -
Some walk becrutched there in the van,
They all look ragged, weak and wan.
See there the colours bravely worn
That speak of Flanders dangers borne;
When those same men in khaki dressed
Were hailed when alien dangers pressed.
Yet now unwanted there they stand
To shame this shameful selfish land,
That spurns and heels its warriors down
Who won for England fame renown,
Who stood when but a dauntless few
And smote the foe face in the dew.

These same now go through London town
Unarmed except for Right's fair crown,
To beg a state that gave wealth to war
For bread and work and nothing more.
Though England's fame fills history's pen,
This darkest blot must stand by them,
To mind the great who wield the power
That in England's day is a murky hour.

ON BEING STUNG BY A BEE

I marvel ever at thee bee
But why are you so frantic?
When ere I step up to your hive
My God! you cut an antic.

I'll warrant all is safe with me
I'll never touch a super,
Why - I've gen you wads of syrup there
My loss! I'm no recouper.

Your hiving is my eye's delight
Your actions I find charming;
But should I move one lift or lid -
Attacks like yours 's alarming.

Yon Queen's a slave in hiving gloom
And you're no better mortal.
I feel skin - my state's no throne
At my distress don't chortle.

For you has nature spread her store
Around for just the taking;
But yet must I for daily bread
Toil on while body's aching.

THE GENTLE DOVE

Precious Dovedale, the gem of Stafford's crown,
Set within a hilly wall of green and rustic brown,
Along thy valley flows the Dove
Pure and gentle the anglers love;
Whose praise they sing in ballad and song
And tell of the trout - in her waters throng.
And of earliest primrose shining there
Beneath the willow yet so bare,
Whose angled boughs in mirrored brook
Are unashamed of naked look.

Where balmy spring brings forth new life
Ere winter's mark has left the heights.
Enfoldened sheep on lowland fells
Will find the spot where crocus dwells
And earliest bite of green that grows
Beside the rills of melted snows,
That tumbling down the steep hillside
Find mother Dove's sweet mossy side.
Then icy waters tell their tale
Of mountain snows and loamless shale.

She quells their turbulent babbling sounds,
Rebukes and softly she them impounds.
Then on her placid way she flows
O'er stony ford thro' verdant groves;
Thro' alien shires who disdain her worth
Besmirch her with their filth and dirt
Till, when she with Trent meets Humber's might
They black and sloughed as darkest night.
Her sporting fry have long since fled
Near where she was born at Three Shires Head.

212

MIDDLE HILLS

Here the summits touch the sky
And misty clouds go rolling by;
Below the valley's patterned green
And blue the lakes that lie between.

Wild song comes from the moors around
And sheep give forth their plaintive sound.
The staring rocks - the pools of brown,
The cairn that marks the topmost crown.

Such awe-inspiring views will greet
The happy tiring wanderer's feet,
Who may take rest where kestrels fly,
And marvel at the changing sky.

Or plunge among some pouring stream
That thunders from the rocks between
Fresh and clear and shimmering cold
That evening sun will turn to gold.

As all this majesty unfolds
A thought the timid heart enbolds,
That He who made the towering land
Made man - His likeness - by His hand.

THE BOMB

They snarl and mouth their hate and gloom
Across a world of little room.
They crow o'er each contraption made
With hearts as green as chinese jade.
Their follies take them wide the mark
Into a pit abyssmal dark,
And there they see with dev'lish eyes
What's hid from folk who are good and wise.
They clamour for the highest stool
And o'er their power vainly drool.
The makers of the bomb may boast,
Pray God that soon in Hell they'll roast!

AROUND THE MERMAID INN

The blue hills reach to touch the sky
Where 'Mermaid' stands supreme;
The wind-borne clouds race wildly by
To leave the skies so clean.
A weary traveller finds the latch
And there inside a rest,
While out, the changing scene portrays
Wild nature at her best.

The sheep for fare range far and wide,
And wild delight is seen
When some young tup risks life and limb
To browse where grass grows green.
The heathered moors their pools conceal
To trap some faltering stride,
The Headless Horseman thence will steal
Upon his lonely ride -
So quick the sun will send a warming ray,
More quickly tho' will mists enclose the day.

THE SILENT TOWN
1936 DEPRESSION

Each lifeless chimney rears its head
A sentinel to toil long dead,
Tumultuous silence mourns the town
That once knew fame and world renown.

The men as lifeless stand and stare
Their scanty frames speak little fare,
Their ragged barefoot children play
Amid those scenes so dark and grey.

Inside each tiny terraced cot
The harassed housewife weeps her lot;
The loaf she marks for each one's dole
And weakly porridge fills each bowl.

Unequal so the struggle seems
An early grave will end her dreams,
While those who rule disdaining spurn -
Away from mis'ry see them turn.

The anguished prayers of those long dead
Whose blood for England's soil was shed
Cry out their shame on those in power,
Who see - but move not from their tower.

ON FRIENDS

When autumn time commands the year
Our thoughts will turn to Leek,
Where friends foregather in the hall
With signs and hands that speak
On mystic law.

Then later Longsdon, where 'The Spinney' lies
We turn an eager gaze;
To sing of times now long sin' gone
While youth stands in amaze
At talents rare.

The strings light-touched by Dougie's hands,
The bass and tenors sing,
Walker, Cornes and Leese give forth
While Boote an arm will swing
In measured time.

And while the moon is high above
We make our homeward way
With mem'ries fond and fonder friends,
To meet another day,
Beneath the sign.

A WISH

On my island there shall be
A tiny place for you and me,
A terrace where to spend the hours
And smell the sweet and varied flowers.

A garden where the lettuce grows
And where the herb so scented blows.
A tiny pond with lilies gay,
Where dragonflies delight the day.

An evening seat where, shaded there,
We watch the merle and mavis pair.
Their evening salutations made
To nest and bough where young are laid.

The morrow with a busy hum
From hives where work has long begun.
Contented with their golden hoard
For winter's dreary days there stored.

As days and years shall pass, we'see
Life's pageant shown, just you and me.
O what a blessing to be there,
Just you and I alone, to share.

AUTUMN TIME, HOW I LOVE

How I love the Autumn time
When twilight's on the lea,
And I haste o'er to Cherry Hill
Where Sally waits for me.

The first mad kiss and fond embrace
Her hot breath on my cheek,
A thousand years of love are pledged
Tho' neither yet may speak.

The worldly woes of life and toil
Fast fleeting like the mist,
While Care and Gloom that doleful pair
Were gone when first we kissed.

O hasten on brown autumn time,
Come twilight on the lea,
Then will I fly to meet my love
The only love for me.

MORRIDGE

High above where moorcock gather,
Where the clouds go hastening by,
Blue the sweet and springy heather,
Blue then black the changing sky.

Then the waters pour unending,
Booming out across the air,
Madly torrents leap and scatter
When the storm clouds empty there.

Wild-wandering winds their pleasures finding
Unhampered by lowland terrain,
Views unbouding stretch for ever
O'er Derby's stony chequered plain.

The heaving hills surround the valley
Where the tiny streamlets flow,
There the wild things meet for shelter,
There the thirsty roedeer go.

Evening cools and mists go stealing
'Prisoning all in ghostly light,
Early gloom the valleys feeling
Lonely hills resist the night.

AMBITION

Youth rides his steed 'Ambition,'
And strains with might and main,
Age looks behind his shoulder,
And tighter grips the reign.

Youth casts about unthinking
And tramples all before,
And foolish builds himself regrets
He'll think on evermore.

Age takes his leisured footsteps
And moves with time and tide,
He knows the pitfalls on the paths
And quiet turns aside. -

But headlong Youth goes madly on
Sage counsel leaves his side;
And those his feet grind in the dust
His vision ne'er will hide.

AND SHE'S MY LOVE

Blood-red the roses hang in June,
Snow-white the fields where daisies grow,
But there's a sweeter flower by far
And she's my love, my dearie O!

The woodbine twines around the thorn
Where shady flowerlets gently blow,
And there I twine my eager arms
Around my love, my dearie O!.

Down yonder vale the cooling stream
Moves softly there so clear and slow,
And peering in the limpid pools
I see my love, my dearie O!.

When evening dims the leafy lanes
With hearts in tune and passing slow,
Where doves are cooing to the nest
I'll whisper to my dearie O!.

AH - SWEET SIXTEEN

Sweet sixteen years is my love yet
Our summer's yet to flower,
And while we may we'll spring enjoy
And live for life's bright hour.

My bosom heaves both night and day
Until I meet my fairest,
Her rosy lips and eyes of blue
My thoughts for her are dearest.

The snow-white thorn will shade our love
Its scent will waft our bower,
The precious moments fleetly fly
As dew bedecks the flower.

As shadows fold the quiet night,
And nature calls for sleeping,
Young love untired throbs with life
No bounds will it be keeping.

ALBION

Across the leagues and leagues of sea
Across the skies so lone and high;
There lies the land where men are free
And for that freedom they will die.

When Roman legions trod her soil
Their eagled banners touched the sun,
So fair the land they deigned to spoil
They named her, 'Lovely Albion.'

But many from the wasted north
In galleys from the lands of snow,
Across her bosom poured they forth
And laid the fair ones deathly low.

The gallic sun its zenith found
Now eager eyes her beauties prized
Her wooded hills, her fertile ground,
Were seen by avid Norman eyes.

The final conflict o'er and done
Her face again shone brightly forth,
Her name the virtues all have won,
Acclaimed from east, west, south and north.

TAKE HEED

Take heed my friend if heights you seek
Beyond your present station,
The ladder's set with traps and snares
That may spell degradation. For example -
Cast pride aside and bend your knee
And grovel 'fore your master,
And when you see his finger crooked
Be sure you move the faster.
Become his slave and let him see
That you'll betray your brother,
And when he spits upon your cheek
Just offer him the other.
And after scrawling on through life
Despised on every han'
Don't be surprised when others point
And ask, 'Is this a man?''.

LINES . . . .
ON VISITING ST. EDWARDS
CHURCH, CHEDDLETON, STAFFS.

No raking spire commands the endless sky,
No garish stone the square-rigged tower climbs;
But here to pause and watch the world go by
While others rest beneath the quiet chimes.

The porchway shields the ever open door
Where time-worn grooves the footway clearly shows,
A pious welcome here the traveller saw
To pour his tale where true compassion flows.

Within is peace no pen can ere relate,
No voice describe with words the joy so still.
This truly is the aesthetic wonderous state
That's felt inside St. Edward's on the hill.

BY THE STREAM

Close beside the gentle streamlet,
Where sweet Blythe runs cool and clear,
There I wander with my dearest,
Pledging love and drawing near,
How the moments pass, so fleeting,
Gathering hours upon the way,
Time stays not - e'en for lovers -
Seize the joys while yet we may.

Can the earth hold treasures rare,
Can the breath make words more true,
Could ought else make pulse race faster
Than love, when heart's trepanned anew,
Tho' the nations rage and conquer,
Tho' the sword may rule the land,
Yet could these be brought asunder
By a loving voice and hand.

IL PENSEROSO

In strength and pride there stands the oak
To fall beneath the woodman's stroke.
The towering buildings touch the sky -
The earth will tremble - there they lie.
The fruitful soil its promise shows -
Now drowned, or as a desert blows.
In Time the present has been seen,
Tomorrow yet may ne'er have been.
The past and present fill the day
The future yet may fly away.
The globe was first the shape to chart
In Nature true is still this art,
The living world is marked by Man
Whose race was run before he ran.
I inward look and ask, am I
Born yet - or yet unborn am I?

ONCE WE LOVED

The roses flowering on the stem
Mean nothing to me now,
Nor feathered minstrels in the glen
A'top their lofty bough.
Another's arms my dear enfolds,
Another's lips will press,
Another's hand so eager holds
My dearest happiness.

I pledged my love to her alone,
She whispered her's to me,
O now my heart feels like a stone
My anguish ne'er will flee.
So soon the flowerlet greets the dawn,
So soon it scents the air,
As quickly does the frosted wind
Destroy the true and fair.

So yet my love must wasted be
And die, ere yet 'twas born,
Just as the flowers that greet the day
Ne'er see the coming morn.
As Fortune holds her every charm
And calls the time and hour,
Her hapless victims forward go
The playthings of her power.

O'ER THE HILLS

With hands clasped tight we cross the hills
To find the brackened lea,
And O what joys we fondly share -
My dearest love, and me.

The mavis fills the woodland glen
His song triumphant rings,
The larkling lifts up from the heath
On joyful notes he wings.

But not for them the burning kiss,
The tender sweet embrace,
Nor eyes that promise future bliss
As pulses madly race.

No 'quake that rents the earth in twain,
No violent skies above,
No desert sun no heaving main
Could part our steadfast love.

IN EARLY AUTUMN

How autumn shows ere summer's flown
While meadows stand as yet unmown,
And fledglings yet remain unflown
While leaves are brown,
Where chestmuts have their blossoms grown
Green conkers crown.

The cuckoo's shout has left the wood
The swallows flee their nests of mud,
And maidens pick the rose in bud
From off the brier,
And evening' skies grow red as blood
Where clouds are higher.

The ending day's are long drawn out,
The fields resound the children's shout,
And fragrant stocks their scent give out
With mighty zest,
Still yet for pleasure some haste about
The south and west.

TO JEAN

When the meadow's full and daisies blow
And buttercups all yellow gleam,
And hawthorn hedge's white as snow
I wander there with lovely Jean.

With her I watch the cooling stream
And O' the blossoms fragrance there,
While gay the lights all dart and gleam
As I am whispering to my fair.

And as she turns to press her lips
To mine, so eager waiting there,
The joy the thrill that burns and grips
Is more, O more than I can bear.

Could we but stay the fleeting hour
Could we but stay with youth and love,
Can man yet find a greater power,
More greater than, more sweet than Love?.

LINES . . . .
ON A TUMBLED COTTAGE

O heap of stones if you could tell
Of those who sheltered here,
What joys your crumbling walls may spell
What sorrows brought a tear.

Some maid, all blushing like the dawn,
A stalwart yeoman's bride,
Across your threshold proudly borne;
Of love you need'st must hide.

What songs the noisy children made,
Who gambolled in the stream,
Of future plans and schemes they laid,
You heard each prayer and dream.

But O, the saddened empty room
That later was their lot,
As poverty, or death's grim broom
Swept them from you - their cot.

LINES . . . .

The tyrant's boot may tread abroad
Reducing all by fire and sword.
But yet he holds the greater power,
Who can produce from earth - a flower.

DOVEDALE

How green and fair thou art, Dovedale,
How clear the singing Dove,
More precious far art thou to me
Than all place else above.

The morning sun thy pearly dews
To amber droplets form,
And soon the mists reveal thy face
All smiling, fresh and warm.

Across thy vale the evening sky
In radiant splendour falls,
And mirrored in thy mossy stream
The crimson light enthralls.

The gentle thrush its evensong
With cadence fills the vale,
And as his parting notes are trilled
There sounds the nightingale.

Above the murmurings of the night
The natives call so clear,
And soft they trip up to thy stream
To sip thy waters clear.

O! sweet Dovedale more sweeter far
As years so quickly fly,
I'll hasten now and on thy green
So peaceful there to lie.

And if a choice I have to place
My earthly cell near thee,
With joy I'll lay me down to rest
A'neath some shady tree,

In fair Dovedale.

LINES . . . .

Before we lift a critics hand,
Before we blame and shout,
First let us wisely inward look
Before we see without.

A DREAM

My dream was one of long transport
To future ages yet unborn,
Would my obscure unlettered name
On some historic shelf be drawn.

Would someone read my rustic line
And feel a homely warmth within?
Maybe to find an answer there
Or perhaps a smile to win.

My muse though rude was a tender flower,
To her commands I was a slave,
Her songs to me were from the heart
More yet from her and more I crave.

Dear reader, if you should trouble take
To scan my verse of rhyming ware,
May you find pleasure at least in part
Among the tales and trials there.